Mingle City

PUBLISHED BY MingleCity, LLC

Other Books
by Michael Baisden

Never Satisfied: How And Why Men Cheat

Men Cry In The Dark

The Maintenance Man

The Maintenance Man II

God's Gift To Women

Raise Your Hand IF You Have Issues

Woman Up!

DON'T LIE TO ME

MICHAEL BAISDEN

PUBLISHED BY MingleCity, LLC

LEARN MORE BY VISITING WWW.MINGLECITY.COM
Find Michael on Facebook or Instagram @ MichaelBaisdenLive

Don't Lie to Me

Published By: MingleCity, LLC
MingleCity.com

Stories used in this book are based on interviews, were penned anonymously, are public domain or were written by Michael Baisden.

Some names and identifying details of certain individuals mentioned in this book have been changed or omitted to protect people's privacy.

Project Manager: Pamela Yvette Exum
Cover Design by Krishna Ko
Book Design by: Stacy Luecker – Essex Graphix

Printed in the United States of America
First Printing
ISBN 978-0-9912698-8-4
Library of Congress Control Number: 1-12536405141

TABLE OF CONTENTS

Start Living With Intention

DON'T LIE TO ME

MICHAEL BAISDEN

INTRODUCTION

Lying is a form of abuse! Anyone who disagrees with that should put this book down and find something else to read! There's no time to mince words or soften the blow of what must be said! Lies destroy relationships! Lies destroy families! Lies can obliterate a person's self-esteem! And lies can get you killed! I know because I was a liar and saw the devastation firsthand!

I'll never forget the day I pushed my wife over the edge! We were arguing about yet another affair she caught me in. We were really going at it! I raised my voice, proclaiming my innocence, and she screamed at the top of her voice, "Don't lie to me!" But this argument would end differently than the previous ones; instead of crying and storming off to the bedroom, she snapped! The next thing I knew, she was coming at me with a knife or some sharp object! To be honest with you, I don't remember. I just know she wasn't just threatening; she meant to cut me!

I quickly grabbed her by the wrist and wrestled her to the floor, and she immediately let the object fall from her hand! As we lay there, she began to tremble and cry. Her emotions triggered mine, and I began to cry too. I knew I had gone too far. And I knew our relationship would be forever changed. She had reached her breaking point!

I pulled her close to me, firmly, lovingly, and she allowed me to hold her. We knew this wasn't us! But the buildup of lies, deceit, and disrespect had poisoned our marriage. Eventually, we stood up and embraced each other. I recall her going to the bathroom to straighten herself out then we sat down and talked. I think she even cooked us something to eat afterward. But that was the kind of woman she was. She never allowed my bad behavior to affect who she was.

To understand how traumatic this was for us, you must first know my ex-wife's history. She was a beautiful, laid-back southern girl from Alabama who her grandparents raised to be a good person and wife. To this day, she is the sweetest, most humble, kindest, most caring, considerate, and most loving woman I've ever known! To push her to have such an emotional breakdown took a lot. And I have to live with the fact that I was the one who took her there.

A couple of months later, we separated. I left to her the apartment, the furniture, the linen, the appliances, the cookware—everything! I was determined to make her transition as comfortable as possible. Over time, things improved, and we decided to spend time together as friends! I'm not sure if I ever told her, but she was the inspiration for my writing my first book, *Never Satisfied: How and Why Men Cheat*? It was my way of healing from all the trauma I caused her and other women. But it was also a warning to other men not to go down the same path.

Shortly after my book was released in January 1995, she shared with me that she had met someone. "I got a position in California, and I want to move there to see if I can make this work," she said. "Can you help me out?" Without hesitation, I told her, "Yes!" I paid for her move to California to be with the man who would become her future husband. And I didn't do it out of guilt—I did it because she deserved it! I loved her and wanted her to be happy with or without me.

I've never shared this story before. It just came pouring out as I sat down to write this introduction. And although this happened nearly thirty years ago, it still impacts me. You never get over hurting good people! But that terrible experience turned out to be the catalyst that put me on a path to transparency. I promised myself never to lie again about whether I had other women in my life—and to this day, I haven't.

It's been a long process to becoming more transparent. It requires maturity, accountability, and a lot of soul-searching. You've got to check your ego and unlearn all the bullshit you were taught by other immature and unevolved men, which is easier said than done when you've been a liar most of your life! But staying on that path of honesty and integrity created a vortex of positive outcomes that have completely changed my life, like having healthier relationships, deeper sexual connections, peace of mind, a solid reputation, and financial success!

But during this evolution over many years, I noticed that the men around me, my friends and associates, weren't changing.

And I wondered, why not? I was 32 when I stopped cheating. Since then, I've watched men and women in their 40s, 50s, and 60s still play childish games, just lying for no reason! They don't even bother waiting for the question to be dishonest. They lie unprompted—they volunteer lies!

And it is precisely because I don't believe most liars will ever change that I'm not going to waste my time trying to understand or expose them. I've written enough about that in my previous books! What I think would be more constructive is to start a conversation about why people are accessories in their own damage. And why don't they seek answers by first looking in the mirror?

Most people think transparency is about being honest with others when the reality is it begins with being honest with yourself! No one can do the work for you—and there are no shortcuts.

To live a more transparent life, you must confront your insecurities and childhood trauma and be prepared to challenge social norms and even your religious beliefs!

So, are you sure you want to go down this road? If so, turn the page, and let's get to work!

People who hurt us aren't always bad people, and they don't always intend to lie and cheat on us. But they do know what they're doing is wrong. They know it's disrespectful. And deep down inside, they know one day they'll be caught. But you know what else they know? They know they can't control themselves from acting in a way that causes damage—and that's the most pathetic part!

1
DAMAGED BY LIES

Before I began writing this chapter, I watched two hours of videos on YouTube about people who caught their partners in the act of cheating. It was painful to sit through, but I wanted to be in the right frame of mind while writing this chapter.

You see, I've never "knowingly" been cheated on, so I don't have those horrible experiences to draw on. But as I confessed in my introduction, I have lots of experience causing that kind of pain, and it's a memory that's unpleasant to relive, no matter how long ago it happened.

But, at least I stopped doing damage at the age of thirty-two. I'm sure I've disappointed and hurt some of my partners in later years, but it was never because of lying about my involvement with other women or my true intentions. That was behind me. But the damage doesn't just come from cheating. There are many other ways of causing women pain, disappointment, and trauma.

To be fair, men get damaged by women too, and I'll address that in a later chapter. But to begin this journey towards transparency, let's focus on the damage most of us can relate to, and that's the damage caused by inconsiderate partners who are reckless with our hearts.

Early in 2021, I was listening to Spotify and downloaded the song *Damaged* by the artist H.E.R. From the moment I heard it, I knew it would become a chapter title in my next book. The vibe was smooth, and the lyrics were powerful! I instantly recognized the music bed; it was from the song "Making Love In The Rain" by Herb Albert, which featured vocals by Janet Jackson. The arrangement was perfect!

I was so moved by the lyrics that I made it the title of the first chapter of this book. And why not? It's precisely because of the emotional damage that results from lies and a lack of transparency that made this book necessary.

The commentary that follows is what I sat down and wrote while listening to the song for the first time. You should play the song while reading this. I promise you it will make the words penetrate more deeply.

WHY DO WE DAMAGE EACH OTHER?
By Michael Baisden

Think about the impact we have on each other as human beings, as lovers, and especially as partners. When our partners aren't properly handled, the impact can be negative. Not in the abstract—we literally can make each other mentally, emotionally, and physically sick, uneasy, or diseased!

And let's face it. People mishandle each other all the time. Yes, I said MIS-Handle because when you open yourself up to someone, you expect them to take care of your emotions and be mindful of your vulnerabilities. We all have them! And when we're deeply involved, those vulnerabilities are exposed.

But, because we're determined to love and make it work, we surrender ourselves to people who don't always understand us or, worse, don't care enough to make sure to avoid going too far, either with harsh words, careless actions, or inconsistencies.

When they don't "take care," damage happens. And what may begin as the usual disappointment and pain escalates to trauma! You might forgive them—but you never forget! And every new episode is a trigger that takes you back to that moment!

Constantly separating over disagreements and a pattern of inconsistency makes you wonder if your partner is trying to sabotage their happiness and yours.

In the lyrics to the song "Damaged," H.E.R. sings:

> *Holding me tight*
> *Loving me right*
> *Giving me life*
> *All night*
> *You could be*
> *Telling me lies*
> *Making me cry*
> *Wasting my time*
> *The whole time*
> *So just be*
> *Careful what you take for granted, yeah*
> *'Cause with me you know you could do damage.*

■ ■ ■

We have a choice to cultivate or diminish: to build our partners up or to destroy them! Yes, the damaged person has a responsibility to protect themselves from further damage. But if you're doing the damage, you must recognize it and correct your behavior or love your partner enough to leave them! Or, as H.E.R. sang in her song, *either learn me or I'm a lesson!*

■ ■ ■

The point of my commentary was to emphasize the lyrics' message in H.E.R.'s song. We can either positively or negatively impact our partner's emotional well-being. Sometimes it goes even deeper. Our behavior towards our partners can uplift them to unimaginable heights or drive them to self-destructive behavior.

I know I'm being redundant, but it's a point that must be emphasized. Each person in the relationship is responsible for their own well-being and happiness, but that shouldn't let them off the hook for knowingly doing damage.

For me, it took a traumatic episode with my ex-wife at the age of thirty-two to put me on the path to being honest, practicing integrity, and being more transparent. But how do you explain men and women in their forties, fifties, and even sixties being utterly indifferent to taking their partners through hell?

Yes, my experience was deeply painful, but it wasn't the only reason I changed my cheating ways. I was determined to be a better person, a better man. And I needed more peace and stability in my life to focus on my goal of becoming a writer. Anyone who knows anything about achieving success will tell you that relationship trauma is not conducive to goal attainment. It's like oil and water!

And finally, I knew being a liar would not only arrest my evolution as a writer but ultimately be my downfall. I was so intensely aware of this threat to my success that I had re-curring nightmares! The one I remember most vividly was a dream about being on stage hosting a relationship seminar, and suddenly, a woman stood up in the middle of the audience and angrily shouted, "You're a liar!" It was terrifying, so much so that I'm writing it in this book over thirty years later! I saw it was a warning not to return to my old ways—or else!

Stepping onto the national stage as a thirty-two-year-old Black man with no counseling license, degrees, or even a certificate, was scary enough! I wasn't about to leave myself open to being called a liar. I was determined to master my role as a relationship expert, or at least a truth-teller! By the time I hit the radio and TV talk show circuit in 1995, I was ready!

My reputation, then and now, is being brutally honest. That's my brand, my rep, my power! And I'll be damned if I do something reckless and that gets taken away from me!

I wondered then, as I still do today, why aren't these motivating factors for everyone? I mean, doesn't everyone want to be successful and beyond reproach? Doesn't everyone want to mature and do away with childish things? Don't we all want healthy relationships and not cause our partners pain? Don't we all want more?

If the answer is yes, then lying and damaging people can no longer be an option! And I don't want to hear any reverse psychology crap about how people can't handle the truth! In reality, liars can't handle their partner's response to the truth. If someone left you because you told the truth about having sex with other people, then they handled it by leaving you! And if they stayed, they made a conscious choice based on the truth! It's that simple!

The title of this book, *Don't Lie To Me!*, isn't just an assertion—it's a challenge! A challenge to be completely transparent about who you are and your intentions—from day one!

So, why is it that people constantly fail to step up? Why do they always seem to choose lies over truth and damage over resolution? What is it about human beings that we can't get out of our way to do better?

I paused to contemplate this most serious question. My answer would become the foundation for, and objective of, writing this book. I took a deep breath and exhaled. Then I embraced my transparency and said what I truly felt out loud!

"Most people are fuckin' cowards!"

HE, Or SHE, WILL NEVER LOVE YOU! AND YOU WILL NEVER BE ENOUGH! A narcissist cuts deep, exposing all your vulnerabilities, and then exploits them. In the end, you won't even recognize who you are anymore.

You'll end up only being an empty shell of the person you once were, convinced that everything that happened is your fault. Run, run, as fast as your feet will take you, then run some more!!!!

— Meko Stephenson

2

DAMAGED
BY A NARCISSIST

It was never my intention to begin this book discussing narcissism, but when I posted about it on my Facebook Page to get feedback on an unrelated project, there was an avalanche of emotions, mostly women posting horror stories about dating men they defined as narcissists. And their comments continued non-stop for well over forty-eight hours.

The post I created read: I should have known he or she was a narcissist when_____. The first comment that caught my eye was from one of my regular followers. I'll just call her Holly. I knew after reading her story that I couldn't write a book about overcoming lies and deception without addressing the issues of narcissism. Anyone who has experienced gaslighting will tell you that, more than any other form of deception, it can be the most emotionally damaging and most difficult to recover from.

Holly wrote:
He broke up with me in the hospital when I was rushed to the hospital after my water broke. I was losing both of our twins! He was upset because my water ruptured at 19 weeks. He dropped off my10yr old son at the hospital and told me I needed to have someone pick him up (nearest family was 5hrs away), all because the stress of me losing OUR babies was too much for HIM to deal with.

Shonda wrote:
Got my window busted out and had to save the mf life because the glass hit a major artery. Another time, this Mf jumped out a tree onto my windshield while I was bringing my daughter home from pre-school. And then there was time when I came up out the pool and this mf was standing at the top looking down at me crying. Should I keep going?

You have to laugh to keep from crying. She's right; that MF was crazy! Now I have this scene stuck in my head of this fool standing at the edge of the pool crying as she surfaced from the water.

Robby wrote:
Imagine your wife wanting you to call in sick to work at the last minute as you're heading out the door so that you can stay at home and watch the kids so she and her mom can go to the mall and go shopping. Then imagine her being mad and not talking to you for a week because you wouldn't.

■ ■ ■

After readings these and other stories, I wanted to learn more about narcissism, so I paused my writing to read articles and watch a few YOUTUBE videos. And what I discovered is that narcissists aren't just liars and cheaters but people who suffer from serious mental disorders. To wake up to that torture every day and to work at trying to please that person to make them love you must be a living hell!

People tend to judge those in relationships with a narcissist as weak and having low self-esteem, which may be true in some cases. But narcissists are talented manipulators who can morph into whatever description you give them of your ideal partner, at least long enough to reel you in emotionally. As a man who was good at playing mind games on women, I know it's hard to recognize when you're being gaslighted, especially if you truly love that man or are at a vulnerable place in your life.

That's why it's important to learn to raise your awareness when dating and not get caught up in smooth talk and gentlemanly behavior that's not authentic or consistent! You must pay attention to anything that seems a little off and then speak up! Narcissistic men don't like women who ask probing questions or have self-confidence. Their goal is to hypnotize her with lies and the illusion of success. So, the less accomplished she is and the less she thinks of herself, the more she will elevate his importance in her life.

But self-aware women aren't stimulated by the depths of a man's wallet. It's the depths of his character and intellect that matter. Unfazed by grandiose stories and material possessions, the self-aware woman stands confidently still when she encounters the narcissistic man who makes her "Spidey Sense" go off! And with the instincts of the characters in Avatar, she stares him squarely in the eyes while he's boasting about himself and whispers sarcastically to herself, "I see you!"

But some women don't have this discernment or ignore the obvious signs because they're intrigued. Narcissists are known to be very charismatic and great pretenders. And what makes them most effective is the uneven ratio of single men to women who are lonely or just plain old bored.

Whatever the reason for letting him in, the narcissist will immediately begin his assault by love-bombing her and take control by undermining every aspect of her life. He'll even try to manipulate her friends and family to get on their good side. Once that mission is accomplished, all hell will break loose! And it doesn't matter the target's age, social status, education level, or physical appearance. Narcissists are calculating and relentlessly cruel! Sadly, most people don't realize just how serious their partner's mental illness is until it's too late!

Patricia wrote:
He tried to kill me...after years of abuse, stalking, gas lighting...he felt we could resolve our issues by getting back together, and married...I refused, he kidnapped my daughter, then beat me nearly to death in front of her. She was 4. He then followed us across state lines with a mission to kill me, and said he would kill us all even my parents and kids from a previous marriage... One day I got hit in the head then woke up in a trunk, being driven to the desert, where he dug a hole...just to scare me he said. I got lucky.

Tanisha wrote:

Narcissistic abuse starts with love bombing and saying and doing all the right things long enough for me to show that I'm smitten. Then comes the devaluing: critical comments, easily annoyed, always busy, one word text responses, and stringing along, acting like I don't matter.

Gaslighting: saying I'm too emotional for wanting to have necessary conversations, denying the intentions previously stated, saying I'm overreacting for asking for accountability. Calling me crazy for not tolerating being disrespected. Stonewalling/Silent treatment: emotional violence, punishing me for challenging his immaturity, and let's not forget the ghosting for days.

Finally, there are the fake promises when I try to leave to bait me back in...then love bombing all over again. A predictable pattern. A mind fuck and plenty of games lies and alibis— total manipulation!

My constant hustle for worthiness, resulting in self-doubt and low self-esteem, which is their goal the whole time...to break me down for his SELF IMPORTANCE.

■ ■ ■

One of the most disturbing aspects of these stories is the age of some men engaged in these acts of torture. Many of them are in their 40s, 50s, and even 60s. You would think they would've sought help at some point. But no! These abusers can't see the damage they're inflicting because they can't stop lying to themselves. You're not a good man and not a player—you're a narcissist!

That's right. I called them narcissists because there's no other definition that explains the behavior of a man who has no control over himself to stop obliterating other people's lives. They come into a woman's world and start stealing things. They steal their time, money, trust, love, self-esteem, and worse, their peace! And they replace it with mental and emotional abuse.

And for those of you who think I'm being too harsh by calling these men narcissistic, read the definition for yourselves. It goes beyond describing someone dishonest—narcissism is abusive and destructive!

Common narcissistic traits include having a strong sense of self-importance, experiencing fantasies about fame or glory, exaggerating self-abilities, craving admiration, exploiting others, and lacking empathy.

I've known at least five men who fit this description perfectly! And they're in my past because I realized they were fucking crazy! I want women to know that we men experience narcissistic men, too, in our friendships and business dealings. But we get to walk away once our night out or meeting is over! I can't imagine what it's like going home to someone with these traits, having to walk on eggshells and constantly being lied to and degraded!

I know that women can be narcissists, too, and I wish more men would step up and share their stories! But the women are the ones who spoke out on my post, so let's deal with it! I wouldn't waste my time attempting to convert these narcissists into responsible, caring people. And women shouldn't lie to themselves into believing they can, either. They need to realize it takes a certain kind of man to repeat this arrogant, unaccountable, and gaslighting behavior!

I advise women to leave these demeaning relationships and never look back! Believe me; it's only going to get worse! Lying to yourself about being able to love the mental illness out of someone is a form of mental illness itself. As a man writing about this, I know it's hard to take my advice, but hopefully, this story posted on my social media page will inspire you to leave before it's too late!

Anonymous wrote:
I have been in three narcissistic relationships and have been financially, emotionally, and physically battered. The last one really took its toll. I had to move 6000 miles away, selling everything, relocating my children, and buying a house, car, furnishings only to find out he was living a double life.

I had to reverse it all, coming back and having to deal with his smear campaign as well as finding it hard to find housing since the market had boomed and there was a housing shortage. I have had to really push myself to stay out of depression. I lived in fear bombarded with threats, disgusting emails and yet I was the victim.

His happy little flying monkeys all on board to make my life miserable. I even went into police protection until everything was sold up and I could get out of the State to return home. Sitting at the airport with the worst anxiety and too scared to go out when he came over to the East looking for me. It has been a horrible time for me.

I walked away quickly from the first one but not without being financially scathed. The second partner and I were together 10 years. That nightmare was full of financial and physical abuse but most of all mental abuse, it was constant lying, cheating, gaslighting, and mind games until I kicked him out only to discover he had a mistress. And then he announced he was terminally ill from his alcoholism and left nothing for his minor dependent children.

Since the passing of my amazing 2002 husband, I have suffered at the hands of these three narcissists. My need to be with a partner meant I was willing to ignore red flags and settle. I admit it to myself now that I was taking men from the clearance rack, not the top shelf. Never again!!! Mind you, men out there are so messed up in my age bracket, I'm over 50. They don't want committed relationships, they want control. They don't want a family life; they want relationships on their terms. They'll love bomb you and then change on you like Jekyll and Hyde.

I think many men are addicted to trauma because of their experiences and they can't have a healthy relationship. Some days I get sad thinking about growing old without a companion but then I pause, take a deep breath, and reflect on what I've been through. I feel a sense of incredible gratitude that I have my incredible sons who seem unaffected by the crap they were exposed to. Perhaps they have learnt to stand up for themselves, to be resilient and not desperate to settle for just anyone.

Please everyone, heed those red flags and set that bar high. Listen to advice of well-meaning family and friends. They see what you are oblivious to because you are under their spell. Educate yourself by reading books and watching videos about narcissistic behavior like I did, it will help you from being drawn into their web! But if you do fall into their trap, run immediately because if you don't, you will be on the scariest ride of your life!

STOP LYING
TO YOURSELF!

Long before we entered our first relationship, the seeds had already been planted to tell and accept lies. Girls are told by their mothers, "All men cheat!" And the Bible is used as justification by scapegoating the cheater with the verse, "The flesh is weak!"

At an early age, young boys observe their lying fathers and uncles being glorified as "Players." While the girls overhear the women in the family, bailing them out with the old excuse of, "A man is going to be a man!"

But today's women aren't tolerating these old double standards. They've gotten hip to the game. Female recording artists, reality TV stars, and social media influencers are leading the charge proclaiming, "Two can play at that game!"

And like fast food chains, lying and cheating have become franchised worldwide. There are no rules to the game. The only objective is to fuck them before they fuck you!

Game On!

3

CULTURE OF LIES

This book is the most important I've ever written! I say this because since I wrote and self-published my first book, *Never Satisfied: How And Why Men Cheat*, back in 1995, things have only gotten worse between men and women. Research shows that people are more frustrated and less optimistic about finding a compatible partner. Americans are having less sex than ever, loneliness is at an all-time high, and people are so damaged from dealing with liars and narcissists most believe they're better off alone.

People nowadays don't seem to even bother with the truth; they lie out of habit. As I said earlier in the book, people volunteer lies. You don't even have to ask a question, and they're off to the races with lies about their financial status, the number of people they're having sex with, about using protection, and about being tested for STDs. And without being prompted on a date, before you can even get through your appetizer, they start lying about wanting to be in a committed relationship! You're thinking to yourself, "I don't even know you fool!"

But why should we be surprised by all these lies? We live in a culture where lying is not only accepted but rewarded. We had a president that lied every day, yet tens of millions of people in 2020 voted to reelect him—74,222,958 of them, to be exact.

The Catholic Church has been lying for decades about sexually assaulting children. And they're still lying about what they're doing to stop it! The fact that the Catholic Church is still in existence is a testimony to how irrelevant lying is—and don't even get me started on all the religious lies, hypocritical preachers, and cheating and lying congregation members! But I need you to stay focused, so I'll move on!

And then there are the other societal lies, such as, "The Good Guy always wins," "God doesn't put more on you than you can handle," "Karma will catch up with the person who wronged you," and the one saying that really drives me crazy, "If you're a good person and work hard, you'll have everything you want in life." It's all nonsense, all lies! Some of the worse things happen to the best people! So, just stop with the lies!

And the culture of lies begins in our childhood: the Santa Claus lie, the Easter Bunny, the Tooth Fairy, the Boogie Man, drinking coffee will make you black, the lie about the lie bumps on your tongue, and the lie about zodiac signs mattering when choosing a mate.

Now, I know my fellow Zodiac Sign fans will feel "some kind of way," but if we're going to confront all the lies and self-lies, astrology lies have to be on the table! Look, I enjoy checking my horoscope from time to time like millions of people do and may have an occasional reading done, but it's purely for entertainment purposes. But speaking from my own experience, I know just as many happy couples who aren't supposed to be "zodiac compatible" as unhappy ones who, according to astrology, should be the perfect match.

While some professionals in the industry will claim you have to factor in the position of the planets, time of birth, etc., I say you're better off factoring in and focusing on unresolved daddy issues, abandonment issues and other childhood trauma, as well as what kind of belief system they were raised in.

I'm a Cancer, and the signs I'm supposed to be most compatible with are Capricorn, Scorpio, and Virgo. But I've had good and bad relationships with women of all zodiac signs. And those relationships didn't fail because of when those women were born but because of their lack of honesty in being able to accept my lifestyle. I could care less about someone's birth sign, and you shouldn't care either. What should matter is their values, standard of living, the kind of household they were raised in, and whether they believe in playing traditional roles or you are planning to customize your relationship.

And let me add this: regardless of all the qualities I mentioned, if your partner allows their jealous and nosy friends into your business, it won't matter what kind of household you grew up in, your birthday, zodiac sign, or how the planets align—it's a wrap!

So, focus on which characteristics matter most and don't put your faith in zodiac signs and other celestial forces. Relying too much on which month and date a person is born will distort your judgement about who they really are. It can make you look for patterns in their personality that don't exist—and that can cause you to overestimate or underestimate their potential! Lies and self-lies create a world of make-believe and wishful thinking. And using these methods wastes valuable time—time that could be better spent cultivating relationships with people you're truly compatible with.

Now that the foundation has been laid, let's get into the main purpose I'm writing this book. I'm passionate about challenging people to be transparent about who they are. Not only transparent with their intimate partners, but with themselves! It's been my passion for the last two years to share with my followers on social media how self-honesty has dramatically changed my life! I guess you could call me a "Transparency Activist!"

Most people don't realize it's the single most important step to living a better life. It can bring you financial success, connect you more deeply with your partners, and, most importantly, give you peace of mind.

But then again, maybe people do understand that honesty and transparency is the key, and they just don't know how to begin the journey.

Well, let me show you the way!

I love women! I love them so much that I tell them the truth. And the truth is, too many of them don't practice accountability, and they deflect on issues that could help them become more self-aware.

Yes, men have issues too, and I'll address those later in the book. But this chapter is about women. So, ladies, ask yourselves, is there work you could be doing to make yourself a more desirable partner, not just physically but mentally and emotionally?

And can I even ask this question without women deflecting?

4

THE MAN
IN THE MIRROR

When I woke up this morning, it was raining outside. I sprung out of bed, rushed to my computer, and began typing. I do some of my best work when it's raining. Thunderstorms are even better. It was the perfect vibe to begin the most important chapter of this book and probably of my writing career. I know that sounds hyperbolic, but it's true! I'm passionate about working with people to help them get through their relationship issues, issues that go much deeper than infidelity. And the solutions to those problems are more complex than just telling people to move on!

I'm not a therapist or a life coach, but I'm a great listener. And like many of you, I've had a lot of life experience. Although I've never been physically abusive to women, as a young man, I was guilty of playing mind games and being a habitual liar, which I stated at the beginning of the book is a form of abuse— and I was one of the best storytellers ever!

And it's because of my history of being a "Bad Boy" I believe I can help people heal in the same way I did by facing my fears and insecurities. I want people to stop hurting each other and be able to trust and love again. But for any real change to happen, you must take that first big step. And that step is towards more self-awareness.

My journey to becoming more transparent didn't begin with my first book; it began with me confronting myself in the mirror. I remember that day vividly. It was a day much like today, cloudy, rainy, and dreary. I was home alone, preparing to go to work. Back then, I drove trains for the Chicago Transit Authority (CTA). I put on my blue uniform and walked toward the bathroom to check myself in the mirror. The mirror inside the bathroom was over the sink at the end of the hallway, so I could see myself as I walked toward it. For some reason, that day, I was more conscious of time and my place in it. And I remember feeling indifferent to going to work that day, something that had been building up inside me for months. Once inside the bathroom, I turned on the light and stared at myself. I took a deep breath as I glanced down at my perfectly ironed CTA shirt and the metal badge pinned to it. Then, I said to myself, "Is this it?"

A lot was going on in my life that brought me to this point. I still hadn't matured. I was still cheating and playing games with women, slacking off on pursuing my goals. I remember playing the lottery every week, hoping I would strike it rich so I could move out of Chicago. I religiously stopped at that gas station weekly on my way to work to gamble my twenty bucks. But I wasn't willing to gamble on myself so I could stop hating my job—and hating myself for becoming just like everyone else at my job who was bitching and complaining but not doing a damn thing to make a change!

Looking at my reflection in the mirror that day was a turning point. I wasn't just tired of cheating; I was tired of being the same person. I know some of you can relate. It's a profound moment in your life where you're determined to have more and be more! And you'll never forget the moment that overwhelming feeling and conviction takes over you! Although it would be two years later before I would leave that job to pursue my career as a writer, my world was never the same. I had moved beyond anger into a new paradigm. My mindset had completely changed. I had changed!

For you ladies who are reading this, I want to say I'm sorry for contributing to so much of your misery before I grew up and discovered myself. I didn't realize until after reading some of the stories from my social media followers who had been damaged by narcissists that I was exhibiting some of those same behaviors, especially gaslighting. That's such a huge problem! Making someone doubt their own common sense is abuse, both mental and emotional.

There's so much emphasis on women making better choices to heal, but men need to heal, too—from being liars and users and being so damn immature. And I will do my best to reach out to our men by taking this message of transparency on the road during my book tour. I will challenge them to be the men you ladies need us to be: to be mature, to be consistent, and to evolve into partners who enhance, inspire, and lead with love instead of coming into your lives and breaking things!

Now, let's talk about how we all can begin to heal from cheating and self-lies—and that journey begins by facing The Man In The Mirror!

If the first words out your mouth when asked about how you're going to improve yourself or how you contributed to your failed relationships is, "What about him, though?"

You're a deflector!

5

STOP DEFLECTING
IF YOU WANT TO HEAL

As a male writer, I never pretend to understand what women want, need, think, or feel. It's always been a critical part of my writing process to reach out to female friends, family members, women who are experts in the field of relationships, as well as my social media followers, to get a full picture of what women are experiencing.

The inspiration to write this chapter on deflection didn't come to me until shortly after I finished the chapter about narcissists. I was taking a day off to research an upcoming chapter, so I created a few posts to solicit comments to add to the book.

One of the questions I posted asked, "Why do women tell self-lies about wanting a 'Good Man' knowing they haven't put in the work? And if women know what they want, why do they constantly settle?"

I'll admit I was trying to provoke an emotional response because let's face it, it's an emotional issue that makes for great content. But I also wanted to be fair, so I posted a similar question directed at men about how they lie to themselves about being "A Good Man." But instead of the women answering the question posed to them, they flipped the script and began attacking the men and deflecting.

Marcia wrote:
Our parents didn't put in the work so why should we have to do anything different. They were happy without being obligated to do anything so we shouldn't be expected to do anything extra that we don't want to.

Eboni wrote:
Women do much more self-work than men. Culture always tells women all the things they gotta do and be. There is a miniscule amount that men are expected to do to be considered a good man. Men get praised for doing the bare minimum. Being a good man is more than being a provider.

Daphne wrote:
Put in the work??? I'm confused   Most single mothers are tired....what work?

Cennetta wrote:
I am confused too. If woman have to work to get a good man. Then she can do better by herself. I thought a man is supposed to be the head of the family and support his family not the other way around. A woman is a man's mate not meal ticket.

Chika wrote:
As long as you do what he defines as good he will keep you but just because you serve his needs does not mean he will do the same. That is my observation. There is such a big deal placed on this 'high value' man when women should be more concerned with someone who values them regardless of his status.

TaNisha Renée wrote:
These comments are making my head spin. I feel like it's the twilight zone reading through here. Like all these women can't be this simple minded 😔 🤦 *Its ridiculous, and it's the more mature women that are killing me with the entitlement... the answer is they not doing anything but probably complaining.* 🤷

■ ■ ■

Look, I'll be the first to admit that men are guilty of doing a lot of dirt, but you have zero chance of becoming a better person and making better choices if you don't take responsibility for your own shit!

Tanisha's comment received the most likes, which was a sign that the deflectors were in the minority but the most vocal. Of course, I knew the question would be engaging, but I didn't expect it to be an emotional trigger. To help add context to the question and get the conversation back on track, I wrote the following commentary.

TO GET THE BEST WOMAN, I HAVE TO BECOME A BETTER MAN

Even as a young man, I wanted to have the choice of the best women, meaning the most attractive (to me), the most intelligent, the most accomplished, the most sexual, the most open-minded, and the most kind. So, I intuitively knew that to have those choices, I would have to develop myself into a man that those kinds of women would find desirable.

Obviously, good women like successful men, so I worked hard to become successful. Women like men who make them laugh, so I developed a great sense of humor.

Good women like generous, fair, and charitable men, so I was conscious of always giving back. Women also like confident men with leadership skills. Fortunately for me, that came naturally, but I still worked to improve those skills and master the art of executing projects and then moving on to what's next.

Even good girls want a man who can satisfy them sexually, so I ate healthily, exercised, and educated myself on a woman's anatomy. But what I learned as the most important was to learn that particular woman's body and then openly communicate about her sexual likes and dislikes to be the best lover—for her!

And let's not forget the importance of being a good

listener, communicator, and honest person—I got that covered! Yes, all these things are what a man should do for himself, but you better believe I see it as a benefit for attracting what I say I want.

So, what actions and work do women think they need to put in other than just saying, "I want a Good Man?"

■ ■ ■

I wanted to challenge my female followers to communicate in detail what they were willing to do to attract the best man— for them! And, as I stated, all the benefits go to the person putting in the work because it improves you, for you and your partner!

But even after reading my commentary, many of them still didn't get it. They refused to accept that their problems began with them! For this group, no matter how clearly you lay out the role they play in creating their own drama, they will never take accountability. They will always deflect. The clinical term for these people is "The Un-nudgeables."

What's sad is that women who choose deflection over accountability are exhibiting some of the same behavior as narcissists. For those of you who are unfamiliar with the act of deflecting, the psychological community defines it as:

When someone turns something around on you, you can call this the word deflection. This is one of the many defense mechanisms in which they knowingly or unknowingly remove their guilt and place it on you. An example of this is someone making you feel bad even though they are clearly in the wrong.

Women should work on fixing this problem so as not to if for no other reason, behave like the men who have hurt them. I realize for some women, it's too late; they will always be the un-nudgeable. They are only willing to see the fault of others, not themselves.

But I want to end this chapter on a hopeful note. Even though many of the initial comments on my Fan Page were deflections, most of them, after my commentary, were from people who understood my point. After the deflectors wouldn't let up, some of my followers came charging onto the thread to defend my position and also to offer some insight.

TaNisha wrote:
I'm seeing woman on here basically that fall in the take me as I am, and I still deserve "This kind of man" I don't see anyone saying they gotta put in work. Looks like a lot of entitlement going on here.

PinkLady wrote:
We cannot and should not assume that "work" means the same to everyone. Everyone doesn't know how to begin the process of healing.

Jones wrote:
I think we understand, the truth is: some of us are delusional and self-righteous. We could put in the work, but that would require us to remember "we're not flawless" and then deal with the woman in the mirror.

Shay wrote:
Amen sister! I don't know where the misunderstanding is. The work that a woman puts in to qualify for a "good man" should be the same work you should want to put in for

herself, the man just benefits.

Willie wrote:
We deserve the equivalent of us...which is what we usually attract.

Carla Sanders wrote:
I think that a lot of women tell themselves that; but they are divided against themselves; meaning their minds eye thinks one-thing and says "I want a good man", but their hearts mind thinks another. Some women want a "Good Man" many don't feel they deserve it, so they create resistance bc deep down inside they don't feel they are good enough or deserve him.

Veronica wrote:
I realized that in order to get the man I had to be the woman that he wanted. Meaning, I had to have all those qualities and some to get that man. I had to put in the work. So, basically, I had to show and prove because I wanted a good man. I wanted to be a good woman for that man but most of all I wanted to be a GREAT woman for myself.

Khalima wrote:
Ladies, this is not the time to shift the conversation. Which is one thing men dislike...unaccountability. We are quick to shift gear and put focus on what the men need to do instead of looking at ourselves.

Dionne wrote:

Yes, if you want a good man you must put in the work to be a good woman. This means taking stock of the great things that you bring to the table and the others that require some work. Take ownership and be honest with yourself and your potential partner. I will never ask more of a man than I'm willing and can give.

■ ■ ■

So many of us have been through difficult relationships where we felt we gave our all without the success we envisioned, which can cause us to be defensive as a form of self-protection. But we need to understand that admitting that we have work to do doesn't imply that men are perfect and don't have to do anything to prepare for their queen—those are independent thoughts.

Gambling is a game better left for professionals. But if you insist on taking the risk, I advise you not to bet more than you can afford to lose!

The same philosophy applies to gambling at love. Your heart can only take so much pain and disappointment before you're emotionally bankrupt. The problem is you never know how much the game cost to play until you're in too deep.

— Michael Baisden

6

RELATIONSHIP RUSSIAN ROULETTE

Most people want to be in a relationship. And most of us want to experience some form of love, or at the very least, a sense of belonging. But to create the love or relationship you want, you must practice transparency, be specific about what that love and belonging looks like, and stop wasting time and taking risks with people who don't want what you want.

For example, when a woman is serious about being married, she has to stay focused on her objective. She can't engage in casual sex with men who have no interest in marriage and expect to be taken seriously. Typically, women suppress their truth, hoping they will change the man's mind with their overwhelming love and great sex, which almost never happens! And even if she communicates her intention to be married at the start of the dating process, if he doesn't "demonstrate" that he's on the same page, then she's living a lie while also allowing him to get away with lying to her!

And even if she's able to persuade him to tie the knot, there's a good chance he'll sabotage the relationship since it was her idea, not his. At that moment, she realizes that her time, emotions, and sexual investment have been wasted, not to mention the financial cost since women are increasingly flipping the bill for dates, co-signing for cars and leases, and investing in their own weddings, receptions and honeymoons.

It's easy to understand why a woman would feel suckered. After yet another failed relationship, she stares at her reflection in the bathroom mirror with her eyes full of tears. "I can't believe you were so stupid!" she angrily says to herself. "You wasted your time—again! And you have no one to blame but yourself!"

The man, who has also invested time and money, doesn't even bother analyzing what happened. He's just glad to be free of her! It's not that he didn't have good intentions. He simply wasn't "into" her. And depending on how things went down, he might snap back since she didn't make her expectations known from day one! Real communication isn't only about expressing yourself; it involves ensuring that what you say to your partner is comprehended.

So, let me make this point loud and clear so that no one can say they didn't understand the rules of engagement. Silence and a lack of reciprocation aren't compliance; it's a sign that you're being ignored! Got it? People who care about you respond to what you say, and they care about how you feel!

The same lesson applies to men who aren't clear about their intentions. It's not enough to speak your truth and check it off your list as mission accomplished. You must follow up, check in, and see if what you're communicating is being responded to with actions. Otherwise, you're just lying to yourself. And why should anyone take you seriously? After all, you let them get away with it!

But wait, it gets even worse! In most cases where marriage is the objective, people don't even communicate their truth about having the expectation of wanting marriage even after years of being together. One person is thinking everything is on track while their partner is getting frustrated and acting out because the man hasn't popped the questions or the woman hasn't asked to go ring shopping. The clueless person is expected to read their partner's mind or interpret their acting out, then deduce what they want them to do. What a waste of time! Why not just come out and say what you want?

I'll tell you why: people fear their truth will scare their partner away! They're petrified of being alone or having to start over. They're so egotistical that they'd rather suffer in silence than allow another man or woman to have them. And to me, that's being a coward!

All lies are cowardice, selfishness, and low down! The error is believing that all lies are spoken when in fact, lies are mostly a series of omissions. When you don't speak up, don't admit what you want, and don't communicate what your intentions are, you're a liar too! I don't care if you're a good person, a good Christian, or someone who doesn't cheat. You're being dishonest. And that causes damage!

Stick around. I'm just getting warmed up!

■ ■ ■

It takes a lot of courage to be alone! And it takes integrity to say, "This is who I am, and this is what my objectives are! And if you don't like it, leave!" It's a tough call to let go of someone you truly love knowing you may not find another compatible partner for months, if not years! Yes, it's that serious!

Every woman understands that it's tough out here on these streets! And every single person knows there's pee in the dating pool! But being alone for a significant amount of time is the price you pay for being transparent. You're going to lose people, lots of people. That's just the way it is!

The same applies to people who just want sex with no commitment. When you're honest about that, people are going to tell you, "Go to hell!" But these days, you'd be surprised by how many people are down with casual sex. All you have to do is download one of these dating apps like POF, Tinder, and Bumble, and you could be "smashing" within hours with no strings attached.

And let's not forget about all the freaks on Facebook and Instagram. People are hooking up on these social media platforms as much as dating apps. So, I ask, why lie about only wanting sex when "sex on demand" is everywhere?! As the old saying goes, "You can get sex when you can eat!"

But even with all the easy access vaginas and penises, people are doing damage by lying! They're lying to themselves and their partners! And although they may have started out just wanting sex, they end up wanting more—much more! Allow me to explain.

Women can get sex with no strings attached 24-7. Do you agree? All she has to do is knock on the next-door neighbor's door or smile at the thirsty guy that's always watching her at 24-hour Fitness. Every woman has a gym stalker who fantasizes about bending her over doggy style while watching her on the squat machine.

But even women who say they only want sex want more. If women were being honest, what they really want is a guy who they like, at least enough to want to kiss during sex, which isn't easy because kissing is more intimate than sex. And women who say they only want sex still want a man who's available to give it to them, especially if the dick is good! That's very different from saying, "I want sex without a commitment."

Follow me on this because it's about to get interesting.

Recently, I had a conversation with a platonic female friend who expressed an interest in one of these "sex with no headache" relationships. The way she characterized her ideal situation was that the man would come over to her place, or she would visit him, and after spending a few hours together "handling their business," they would return to their respective homes. Okay, cool! I thought.

But then I pressed her.

"So, how often do you want to see this man?" I asked.

"Once or twice a week," she replied.

"How often do you need to talk to him?"

"Not that often. A few times a week would be enough."

"Okay," I said. "Are you cool with him having other partners?

"Of course not!" she said with indignation.

I stared at the phone as if I couldn't believe what I was hearing.

"So, let me get this straight. You want a fuck boy that you don't have to talk to, who's at your beck and call, and you don't want him to have sex with anyone else?"

"Exactly!"

"Some people call that a committed relationship!" I said jokingly. "Why not just have him move in? At least you'd have a penis on standby when you need it."

"Oh, no!" she said, sounding annoyed. "I need my space!"

Just then, I got a call from my partner. I excused myself and told her I would talk to her later. I shared that story with my partner that night, and I've been sharing it with just about everyone I talk to ever since, just to get their feedback. I kept her identity anonymous, of course, but her story was the kind of half-truth rarely discussed. And by half-truth, I mean people tend to speak the truth about what they want, but their words contradict what they say they want from the other person. It's not the complete truth. It's what I like to refer to as "grey area communication." It's saying enough to clarify your needs but leaving enough ambiguity to wiggle your way out if you change your mind. And that's cool, too, just don't call it being transparent!

I know some will say, "How is she not being honest? She's said what she wanted upfront!" And my response is, "She may be communicating honestly, but she's not being transparent!" Allow me to explain the difference as I see it.

Honesty is simply responding to a question truthfully or sharing a story that, in principle, is true. Honesty doesn't reveal any details except in the specific area of the question being asked.

However, transparency is telling the whole truth beyond what's being asked. It means volunteering all the relevant information that allows the person you're speaking to evaluate whether they want to choose you or not. Another way of looking at transparency is telling your partner everything you'd want them to tell you, even if you didn't ask them. In short, transparency is unsolicited truth!

You see, I know my friend wants more than just sex. But she doesn't know how to be transparent about everything she wants with sex to include and the rules of engagement. And she's not alone—most people are half-steppers! Most people are only used to engaging each other on the surface, which can create problems down the road and waste lots of valuable time!

People always say communication is the key, but my question is, communicating on what level? The "raw truth" is the only truth any of us should be interested in hearing, not the truth that's easiest for people to digest. And not the truth that makes it more likely that someone will accept us.

My female friend would have been more transparent had she said, "I want a man to love me, care about me, and be available for me but won't make me feel smothered. And I want him to love only me because I only want to love him! And maybe one day we can live together after my son graduates, but not right now! I just want someone around who I can grow with and who won't make me feel obligated to talk to him or be with him all the time."

Now, that's what honesty and transparency sound like! Of course, knowing my friend better than you, the reader, gives me an advantage in deciphering her expectations. Still, I can see right through most people's bullshit and insecurities from the moment the conversation starts! People aren't as complicated as they think they are. We all want the same things; to be loved, to feel valued, to feel special, to be accepted, and to be understood.

When you start living a more transparent life, you enhance your powers of discernment about what people mean even when they're not saying the exact words. You're more empathetic and intuitive because you used to be that person who constantly lied to yourself. And finally, by becoming transparent, you accept that living in your truth means having fewer friends and a much smaller dating pool.

But creating an authentic and stimulating relationship is not a numbers game—it's all about timing. I'm not talking about timing that conventional thinkers on so-called seasons, but opportunities that you manifest by living in the moment, with purpose and intention. You don't care about the pool size because you're confident that what's meant for you will gravitate to you. You are not put in motion by some mysterious cosmic force but because you're living every moment of your life as your authentic self!

Here's a quote I frequently post on my Facebook Page that expresses this sentiment perfectly: "What's for you can't resist you—and what resist you isn't for you!"

NOW THAT I'VE GOT YOUR ATTENTION— LET'S GO DEEPER!

The most damaged woman isn't the celibate one who stays home night after night binge-watching Netflix, but the one constantly out in the streets meeting new men and going out on dates. Don't be wrong. I'm the first to encourage my female friends to make themselves more available and take chances. After all, dating is a numbers game. But those dates should only be with men who meet your standards, and not just physical dates—if a serious relationship is your objective.

But some women are so desperate for a date they don't bother vetting the man with a few simple questions that would reveal his true intentions. Of course, most of these dates end up being a waste of time, often resulting in inappropriate sexual advances. One of my social media followers I interviewed for this chapter shared a story about a recent date, which is the perfect example.

She accepted a date from a man she worked with at a New York hospital. He was her superior but in another department. He invited her out to his home in upstate New York, which was a three-hour ride from her apartment in Queens. After driving around lost for an hour because of bad directions, she arrived at his home.

She described it as a gated mansion. She went into detail about how beautiful the grounds were and the house's contemporary design. She was clearly impressed.

He greeted her at the door with a friendly hug. Once she was settled in, he took her on tour. She went on and on about how nice his place was, not in the normal way someone would talk about a home they were visiting, but similar to how you would describe a house that a realtor was showing you to purchase. But I digress!

Immediately after the tour, he offered her something to drink, which she accepted. After pouring her a glass of wine, they went into the living room and sat on the sofa.

So, there they were, alone at last in his beautiful home, spending quality time getting to know each other, or so she thought. Instead of relaxing and engaging in small talk about work or each other, he suddenly springs up and says,

"You mind if I take a shower?" You already know where this is going, right? She replies, "Not at all!" He invites her upstairs to his bedroom suite and says so they can talk while he's showering. Again, she accepts.

He strategically sits her in the bedroom where she can see into the master bathroom. While they're talking, he disrobes and wraps a towel around himself, ensuring she gets a clear view of his dick. Embarrassed, she looks way, at least that's what she told me.

After his shower, he comes into the bedroom, where she's sitting in a chair at the foot of the bed. Once again, he flashes his package. I guess he wanted to make sure she got a closer look. Then to no one's surprise but hers, he asks for a massage, which I recall her saying she agreed to.

Now is where the story gets interesting. After her driving for 3 hours, taking her impressive tour, sipping on a glass of wine, chillin' in a man's bedroom while he showers and flashes his junk, and then giving him a massage, she is offended that he expected sex—and that he was frustrated when she declined.

Long story short, she spends the night, they sleep in the same bed spooning without having sex, and his dick is hard all night! The next morning, he's short with her, and while he gets dressed, he mumbles loud enough for her to hear, "I can't believe this shit! I can't believe we didn't have sex!" Within 30 minutes, he shows her the door. But that's not the end of the story.

Two weeks later, they decide to go on another date. This time, she invites him to stay overnight at her place. They go out on a dinner date, which, according to her, turns out great. Then they return to her apartment and prepare for bed. Once again, Mr. Chippendales takes a shower and flashes his dick! And again, she's offended.

They go through this same torturous routine of kissing and snuggling but no sex. And to no one's surprise, he wakes up the next morning mumbling to himself once again about how he can't believe she led him on and that he's shocked they didn't have sex.

Now, maybe I should have established at the beginning of the story that both these people are professionals over 50. But this is the kind of nonsense that's happening all over the world because people are lying to themselves and their partners about what they want and what they expect.

In my opinion, they were both fools! But she was the biggest fool of all. I'm not calling her a fool just because she went to a man's house on a first date. We're all grown! I'm calling her a fool because she drove three hours to his house in upstate New York—on a first date! And she played herself by not communicating to him that her objective was a committed relationship and, ultimately, marriage.

This is what happens when you lie to yourself about what you want or suspend your standards! It's an act of desperation, believing you can manipulate a man into committing to you by using sex as leverage. Women who behave this way are starving for companionship and attention and are willing to play "Relationship Russian Roulette" rather than creating an interview process to eliminate undesirables!

And these are the same women who call their girlfriends after these disastrous dates complaining, "These men ain't shit!" Well, maybe you ain't shit—for constantly dating without being transparent!

Like I always say, when you love women, you tell them the truth! And the truth is you're responsible and accountable for your choices. When you know better, you do better—and now you know deflection is NOT healing!

CAN A "GOOD MAN" BE A LIAR?

I wrote my first book, Never Satisfied: How & Why Men Cheat, *to expose the games men play, the pain it causes, and for men to stop lying before it catches up with them.*

My second book, Men Cry In The Dark, *told the story of four friends, a single father dealing with the narcissistic mother of his child, a Black man dating outside his race, an older man dating younger women—for all the wrong reasons, and a cheating man who didn't realize he had a good thing until it was too late!*

The Maintenance Man *was my third novel. The main character, Malcolm, was a male prostitute—and gigolo. It's a sexually explicit novel that transports the reader into a world where powerful and wealthy women use men as sexual objects. But the underlying story is about how Malcolm lied about who he really was to the woman he loved—lies that could cost him everything!*

Those are just three of my eight books, and the lessons are all the same—lies cost! And no matter how hard you try to hide them, the truth always comes to light!

7

MEN COULD HAVE IT ALL IF THEY WOULD JUST BE HONEST

Sometimes I just want to shake the hell out of men when I watch how they manage their relationships and scream, "Snap out of it, you idiot!" Grown men in their forties, fifties, and even sixties are making up stories and lying about things they don't even have to lie about. They lie about being married, about not having girlfriends, about how many sex partners they have, about using protection, about what they do for a living, how much money they earn, how many kids they have, and how many baby mamas come with those kids.

But what's so crazy is men are lying for no reason! If a woman wants to be involved with you, she's going to be down for whatever if she is that into you! I'm hesitant to use that expression—but it's true!

Listen, fellas, let me put you onto some serious game. There's a woman out there looking to be with you, regardless of your situation, if they're feeling you!

There are plenty of women who will deal with married men, men with girlfriends, men with multiple sex partners, men who've been in prison, and yes, men who are living in their mama's basements! If you're the man she wants!

If this weren't true, there wouldn't be millions of women dealing with men who fit this description. And we all know women who either have been or are currently involved with men in these situations. There's a good chance one of those women is in your presence right now. Hell, it's probably you!

The problem I have with men who lie to take advantage is the same problem I have with some women. They're too impatient to wait for the quality of men they SAY they want. They're unwilling to put in the effort to be a better woman to increase their options. And they, too, damned immaturity and unevolved to live in their truth to give a man a choice.

Men must give women a way, a chance, an opportunity to accept their situation instead of leading with lies. I think most guys would be shocked at how many women would be okay with their situation! The woman you think will have a problem with your open lifestyle might be down with having threesomes. She may not care about you being married. And she may not want you to get a divorce. Her attitude might be, "Handle your business and take your cheating ass home!"

But instead of being straight up and taking the chance to have it all, too many men fall back into their habit of love bombing, selling fantasies, and lying.

What's so ridiculous is nine times out of ten, these

women know they're lying and deal with them anyway. As I said, "If she's really feeling you." The story you made up about your marriage being on the rocks was justification she used to do what she already wanted to do!

It goes without saying that some women won't accept your truth. Many women have their ideal relationship locked in their minds of being in a monogamous relationship or marriage and living happily ever after—there's no way they're going to be a cheating man's side piece. But there are millions of women coming out of long-term relationships and bad marriages, and the last thing they want is commitment. The man who already has a partner may be just what the doctor ordered!

And if the man is attractive enough, has enough money, or they have strong sexual chemistry, these relationships can last for years, if not decades, which many do. Never forget, fellas, she's there to get hers, too—it's not all about you!

So, it's clear some women are open to a man's truth about having other partners. He could have his cake and eat it too but simply be telling the truth. So, what's stopping him? Well, that would take another chapter, but I can break it down into two main reasons.

One reason men lie is they feel it will reduce their options. In other words, lying allows them to sucker more women into believing they're a "Good Man," which is immature and low. But my challenge to men is, why not fix the issue causing you to feel your options are reduced? Let's keep it real. If you're not willing to grow up and be honest because your pool of women to choose from is too small, maybe you should move to Atlanta, Houston, or Los Angeles, where the ratio is 10-1, and that's being conservative.

But here's the crazy part: even men living in these cities where the ratio of women to men is ridiculously high are still lying to women! So, it has nothing to do with reduced options. It's simply a lack of character. It doesn't matter if the ratio was 100 to 1.

This point reminds me of a conversation I had with a small group of friends during our trip to Egypt in 2022. It was late at night after quite a few drinks, and the subject of men being dishonest came up. One of the single men stated that he would never let the women he was dating know about each other.

Now, let me share a few details to give you a complete picture of what I was dealing with. The man who said this was an attractive gentleman in his mid-forties, financially well off enough, and he described himself as "kinda single," meaning he was single when his partners weren't around. Anyway, he told the group he'd never be completely honest about having sex with multiple women. And then went on to say to me, "You can afford to tell women the truth because you're Michael Baisden."

Everybody's mouth dropped. I laughed and responded, "I've been honest with women since I was driving trains for the CTA on the South Side of Chicago." I told him, "So, now, what's your excuse?"

You may recall I shared the story in the introduction about the pain and humiliation I caused my wife and other women in my life when I was younger and how that put me on a path to transparency. But I was in my early thirties when I woke up, and I wish I had come to my senses sooner. But this man was knocking on fifty and still behaving like a Wannabe Playa!

It's sad that so many of our men lack the maturity to just be themselves. Instead of being transparent and putting their cards on the table, they deflect so they can weasel out of being honest from day one. And they don't lie to protect their partners from being hurt. They lie to keep their partners from leaving their weak assess or exercising their option to date and have sex with other men. Any other excuse they give you is bullshit!

And that's why most men lie; they want to take away your choice while exercising their option to do whatever they want to do. Then men try to use reverse psychology by claiming women can't handle the truth. Well, that's also a bunch of nonsense. It's not that women can't handle the truth. It's men who can't handle women's responses to their truth. Never forget that. Write it down because you will need it when the games begin! First, he'll lie to himself to convince himself that he's lying to protect you, and then he'll lie to you with a clear conscious.

The work that it takes to overcome self-lies can take decades. I should know because I'm still doing the work that began at the age of thirty-two. That was over 25 years ago. But that work could never have begun if I didn't start being real with myself and admitting I was immature, insecure, and weak!

That's right. I said "weak" because lying to yourself and others is a character; WEAKNESS! And just like a weak muscle, you must strengthen it; you have to work it out! Practicing transparency is the only way it will become second nature. In the same way lying is a habit with some men, you must make a habit of being transparent.

And a man shouldn't wait for the first date to be honest. Tell her during the first phone call, as I do. If I'm involved with someone else, I'll tell a woman I have a partner, or two, if that's my current situation. And I'll be specific about the status of those relationships and whether I plan to continue seeing and being intimate with those women. Now she has the choice to continue to get to know me better or keep it pushing!

Who has time to be peeking out the window, checking to see if the girl is pulling a drive-by? Or having to turn your phones over or off during a date? Why should a grown man be stressing over hiding another woman's panties and cleaning up strands of a weave on the carpet?

Telling the truth means you can have it all without the drama and headaches of being busted. No more attacks on your reputation or worries about a woman embarrassing you on stage during a speech or making a scene at your wedding. And no more distractions from your business ventures which require your focus to be successful.

As with every chapter, I posted these issues on my social media page to get some perspective from women and men to get their take on why men lie when they could have it all. They posted some great comments.

Shun Taylor wrote:
Yes, I totally agree! I respect you more when you are not just honest but transparent. It creates a safe space for me to be vulnerable in. There are a lot of things I am okay with...if I am given the opportunity to make my own decision from the jump.

Men say: To love them is to respect them! Well, if that's true, BE HONEST because that will get you the ultimate respect with most reasonable and rational women!

Wanda Bradford wrote:
Communication possibly could remedy a lot of unnecessary problems. When you're honest about your needs, desires, and expectations it will allow a person to decide how they want to proceed with the relationship.

Vanessa Corbin-Cunningham wrote:
I totally agree! There's no reason for lying. Just be up front from the beginning. What a lot of men don't realize is that there are a lot of us women that want the same things they want sometimes. But they choose to lie thinking that that will get what they want faster.

April Johnson wrote:
And then they make it worst when they CONTINUE to lie when we already know the truth.

Willy Anthony Nickson wrote:
Yes we could..... BUT you can't have it all with ALL women. Often the risk of losing a desired woman because of truth will cause a person to lie or withhold information. I think this is formed in a man's youth. Most girls are taught to be "good girls" so when they start dating and becoming sexually active.... they often embrace that persona. They will often only engage in sexual activities if the young man paints a picture that allows them to continue to believe they are good

girls. i.e. "He says he loves me", "He says he is going to marry me, he says I'm special, he says I'm the only one", etc.

Unfortunately, this trains the young man that in order to be successful romantically, you have to tell a woman what she wants to hear—and it often works. Telling a woman the whole unadulterated truth will often cause him to lose a woman he desires if she doesn't embrace or agree with his honesty.

The big problem is that most men never grow up from this thinking, mainly because it still works...especially on women who suppress their own truth and are still playing the "good girl" role. We ALL need to be 100% honest and we would spare ourselves a LOT of disappointment.

■ ■ ■

I ask you, what kind of man wouldn't want peace in his life that comes from being honest? What kind of man doesn't want to grow up eventually? And what kind of man doesn't want to be able to look at himself in the mirror and say with conviction, "I'm a good man and a man of integrity!"?

I'll tell you what kind of man doesn't want that: the kind who doesn't have anything of substance to offer. He can only pique a woman's interest through love bombing and selling fake monogamy. He can't stimulate her mind. He can't engage her in politics, travel, or ideas about how to improve her business. And he doesn't set a positive example that challenges her to want to be better.

In short, he can't provide a damn thing of value! All he has to offer is lies! And this is the kind of joker who has the audacity to be the loudest on social media and in women's faces proclaiming, "I'm a Good Man!" Fool, go sit down somewhere!

Can you claim to be a man if you're unable to provide resources? While some women may value financial resources, others have a greater need for mental stimulation, spiritual growth, career support, and sexual pleasure. Or all of the above!

But it's presumptuous for men to expect that every woman is after their money, especially since it's mostly single women purchasing homes, starting businesses, and travelling internationally.

With that being the case, men are being challenged more than ever with the question women are desperate to have answered: "How can you add to me?"

8

ARE YOU A MAN IF YOU CAN'T PROVIDE?

So, what defines a man as being "a man"? I think most people believe that being a man begins with taking responsibility for your actions. It also means being able to provide for yourself and your family. But society teaches us that if a man can't provide, he's useless. And that's true regardless of the culture you're raised in. But my question to women is, "Provide what?"

The assumption is that providing means bringing financial resources to the table. And let's be honest, having an income is important. It's not a matter of being rich or making six figures. However, a man should be able to keep a roof over his head and pay his own bills; otherwise, why should any woman take you seriously?

But let's assume this hypothetical man has a good job that allows him to pay for his essentials, owns a decent car, and has enough disposable income to date. Would most women consider him for providing enough? Again, if we're being honest, the answer is no! Some women might be satisfied with that but not most.

Most women are not impacted by a man's ability to take care of his living expenses. Yes, she should appreciate him taking her out and spending his hard-earned money on dinner dates and the movies, but that's not really adding to her life, is it?

Again, it's appreciated, but dinner and movies aren't most women's idea of bringing something to the table. Men must consider that women are paying their own bills and being the custodial parent of their children and the primary caretakers for sick and elderly parents. They have their hands full financially. So, any man who considers paying his own bills as "holding it down!" is a joke! You can label that as surviving but not providing.

Even when a man is bringing a six or seven-figure salary to the table, that only has value to women who aren't financially stable or ones looking to be taken care of. Again, I'm not implying that providing money isn't important, but it's just that resources are often not what women complain is missing in their relationships.

Men only need to put the shoe on the other foot and ask themselves what they want a female partner to add to their life, and the answer would come more easily. Unless you're a man struggling financially, a woman providing money isn't that big of a deal to you. It's not as if most men are dating six-figure women anyway or vice versa.

According to the U.S. Department of Labor, Black American men earn an average of 47,944 annually, Hispanics 44,772, Whites 61,984, and Asians 74,984. So, ladies, if you're wondering which men have the best jobs and highest future earning potential, you better get yourself an Asian man! And by the way, less than .05 percent of American men earn over one million a year, so good luck with being a gold digger!

My point is once both parties demonstrate the ability to pay their living expenses, providing things of substance comes into play. So, fellas, get yourself unstuck from this belief that providing money is what it means to be a man. You're about to learn that you're missing the big picture!

This fixation on providing money is exactly what I expected when I posted a question on my social media pages asking men to chime in on the subject. But instead of looking deeper within themselves to share other qualities they had to offer, they focused squarely on the dollar signs!

So, let me show you how I framed the question, then you can decide for yourself if the men are deflecting or answering the question. This is what I posted:

Too many men tell the self-lie about being a "Good Man" when they're not honest, response-able, or providing.

Below are their responses.

Bill wrote:
At this point I just take care of me. I never had children so none of that providing should be expected from me. I'll continue to work, pay my own bills, do my own cooking, cleaning, laundry, and enjoy the peace I have when I come home. Basically, I'm keeping my money in my pocket!

Stan wrote:

It's always about money with today's women. Why should a man have to provide for dinners, movies, and all the woman has to do is look good? F**k That!

Anthony wrote:

These strong and independent women need to make up their minds, one minute they're saying they don't need a man and in the same sentence they're talking about a man needs to step up and provide. I work hard for this paycheck, and I live a pretty good life. Why should I be expected to provide for anyone other than myself. And these women wonder why men don't want to date, dating cost.

Shawn wrote:

There's too much pressure on men to always come up with the funds to be in a relationship. We all have financial responsibilities, so why should the man be expected to fork over his hard-earned money before he even knows if she's "The One"?

Rich wrote:

The selfish comment by these women is typical! All they care about is what a man can do for them, what he can buy. They want money for rent, cars notes, and for you to pay to get their hair done. Money, money, money! That's all they're about! I can hear that damn O'Jays song playing in my head right now! Well, they can keep the coochie and I'll keep my lights on! How about that?

■ ■ ■

In fairness, the word "provide" has historically been understood as providing money and all the comforts that come with it. But it must be said that their own conscience has some of these men jumping to conclusions. I never said anything about money in my post. I left out financial providing on purpose to allow them to fill in the blank.

I need men to understand there's more than one way to provide, more than one way to complement your partner, and more than one way to add to a woman's life. One way is to provide your perspective and worldview. Women love it when their man can share insightful opinions about politics, finances, and world news and offer a male perspective on relationships.

Women need men to provide emotional support when adversity hits and they need a shoulder to lean on. And by the way, providing affection and love are also valuable to women, especially when it's given without expectations and with consistency.

And consistency goes hand in hand with creating stability. Women need to know their man is going to be around for the long haul and not take off at the first sign of trouble. Women want me to provide a vision for the relationship and then articulate clearly how she fits into it. And this should be done without constant breaks up, unresolved arguments, and drama from outsiders.

You know, you always hear people talking about how women need to be a man's peace. Well, men need to be a woman's peace too! Having peace of mind is a two-way street! Both partners must be dedicated to creating harmony and keeping outsiders out of their business.

Finally, men need to provide engaging conversation. This is the number one issue women have from around the world! They complain to me, "Men don't have anything to talk about," and "They just hold the phone expecting you to carry the conversation!" And then there are the complaints about men constantly texting instead of calling. But today's woman wants to talk to her man, not read texts—she yearns to hear the soothing tone of his voice and share how her day went. The ability to grab and hold her attention when talking on the phone or in person is everything to a woman!

The quality, length, and depth of your conversations are the single most important factors in measuring the potential for a relationship to be successful. Sexual chemistry is great! Physical attraction is necessary and appreciated! But if you can't talk before, during, and after sex—without the TV on and with only you two in a room, and if you can't talk about any and everything—you're wasting your time!

I know there are "Good Men" out there who understand the importance of providing more than money. The men I know personally who are happily married certainly do! I think those of us who know better should make it our mission to spread the word.

Being the die-hard optimist I am, I wanted to give the good men on my social media platforms an opportunity to demonstrate to women they understand what it means to provide wholistically. I thought about what I could post that would get the attention of the men who truly loved their partner and were also emotionally intelligent. So, I created the following post, and it read: *Fellas, how do you add to, enhance, and complement your woman?*

DON'T LIE TO ME

Their words were articulated beautifully!

Laurin Nichols wrote:
Every situation is different, but this is what worked for me. My wife and I have been together for 30 yrs now. First my wife and I both had young kids. And I was a father to all the kids equally no step daddy B/S.

Second there was never any your bills and my bills. All the money went to the bills first. Then 401k and savings. Third when we got married, she never had to worry about anything. Whatever problems came up she knew I was there to handle it.

And I always went out of my way to make her feel special every day from the beginning to now.

Richard Larochelle wrote:
A random kiss in public, whisper in her ears how great she looks or how I love her perfume. A random sexy text in the middle of her workday.

H Ray Best wrote:
I listen to her & learn from her, I love giving her compliments. I ask her in a nice way to things for me, instead of telling her to do things for me. I open doors and pull out the chair for her, always let her order first, chivalry isn't dead. I've worked on using my inside voice instead of screaming. Positive delivery and respect go a long way.

James Sneed wrote:

Being her biggest fan even when she feels like she's failing, pointing out the positives will help keep her motivated. Seeing what I can help with take some of the stress off her plate and or just being a listening ear. Showing her she's appreciated.

Chad M Owens wrote:

Ask about her day and listen when she talks about it. Constant reassurance through difficult times. Let my actions speak louder than words with consistency.

Ron Riley wrote:

I tell her I love her every day. Whatever challenges she may face I let her know we will get through it together. I not only ask how she is doing physically but mentally. I've learned to just listen to her about whatever she wants to express.

Boderick Johnson wrote:

I compliment and support her goals, dreams, and ambitions. Provide the feedback to help keep her grounded and focused on the task at hand. Feed into her emotionally, spiritually, and financially if needed. Be the Ying to her Yang. Most importantly I pray for her and with her. 🙏

Chase Gore wrote:

I follow the golden rule. I treat her as an equal. Complimenting her physically, emotionally, and mentally. Listening attentively; encouraging and helping when/where I can, and empathizing and holding her, when I can't. I

*help to keep things in perspective. I always add humor to
break up a busy day. Always looking at her in complete
awe and appreciation. Sprinkled with lots of romance, and
never forgoing the little things. Always keeping my word and
following through.*

■ ■ ■

The responses by these men made me proud. It gave me
hope that some men actually "get it!" Too often, we men think
opening up emotionally is a sign of weakness. But that's not
true! It's a sign of strength and maturity for a man to say to
his woman, "I love you!" in front of his boys. And it's not a
weakness to cry with your partner when you're both going
through hell. Or maybe you've cried tears of joy, whatever! Be
a man, and let it out!

We must, as a society, do a better job of redefining what
strength is and move away from these archaic definitions of
what it means to provide—and what it means to be a man.

Being a man means more than opening your wallet. It
means opening your heart. It means taking a chance to be
vulnerable to experience a deeper connection, a deeper love.
Complementing your woman isn't about spending money
but investing time. And adding to a woman's life isn't about
impressing her by constantly grinding to get ahead but about
stopping and smelling the roses and providing her with your
undivided attention, and being present.

Put all that together, and a man can provide his woman
with what she treasures most—a sense of security.

9

SHOULD A WOMAN HIKE THE BALL TO A LIAR?

When you're the quarterback, all eyes are on you. Every game, every quarter, every play. Once the ball is snapped, you control the outcome. Whether the play results in a touchdown, a first down, or a fumble depends on how effectively you play your position. If you win, the team wins. But if you fail as the quarterback, all the blame goes on you.

Being the man in a relationship is much like being the quarterback. It's a position that comes with a lot of pressure and responsibilities. You've got to stay cool under pressure, adapt when the play breaks down, and know when to take a sack instead of making a mistake that could cost you the game.

But the most important aspect of being the quarterback is being trusted by your teammates to call the right plays and not to hurt the team. Because without trust, no man can be an effective leader. And without respect, he won't be able to continue leading or ever be given the authority to lead in the first place!

Some men believe the role of leader is something that is ceased or you're entitled to because you have a penis. But intelligent women, and women who grew up with examples of strong fathers, require a demonstration of leadership before they submit.

I define submission as a woman who trusts her man to take the initiative in creating a vision for their relationship, his life, and their family—if that applies. Submission, to me, is about a woman allowing her man to take the lead when it comes naturally for him to do so. That's an aspect of being compatible you better consider when choosing a partner. Good leaders have a record of successfully leading, beginning with how they lead in their own lives. Never forget that!

Whether it's a man who lacks leadership or other deficiencies, the game begins to wear thin. Some women can put up with more shit than others but eventually they wake up—every woman has a breaking point! And this is the situation many women find themselves in due to men's lies and recklessness. Once the trust and respect are gone, a woman will stop relying on the quarterback to make decisions, take off with the ball, and take her chances. Better that than to be constantly disappointed by a man who refuses to lead or, worse, is incapable. Either way, she knows the bills must be paid and the children have to eat. And so, the game goes on!

■ ■ ■

Come to think of it; maybe the football metaphor is useless. Women today don't have the same expectation for men to take the lead, at least not like they used to. So, here's a more contemporary metaphor: relationships should be more like doubles in tennis and volleyball. They both bring talent and strength to the game. One partner may be a better server, the other a better defender, but they're both equal in importance to winning.

But regardless of which sports metaphor you relate to, it all boils down to trusting your partner to make the right play consistently! It's not so much about trusting a man to be the only one who leads but trusting him to be a good decision-maker. Not only that but can you trust him not to get in the way of your success? A man who lies and cheats constantly worries about his woman taking her revenge by doing the same thing to him. And that insecure mindset can cause him to act in ways that can destroy the woman's opportunity to pursue her dreams.

An example is when I was hosting my national radio show in Dallas. I solicited authors to come to the studio to discuss their books on a feature I called *Living Your Dream*. Typically, all our interviews were by phone, but my producers talked me into doing a live interview with this author. Based on their conversations and her content on the internet, they thought she had the potential to become a regular on the show, which is a win-win for everyone involved.

Well, on the day of the interview, she was running late. When she finally showed up at the receptionist's desk, it was ten minutes before airtime, and she wasn't alone. Now, keep in mind, she was our very first guest on this new feature, so I advertised her appearance coming on the show all week.

I was up against the clock, so I sent my producer to escort them both in—but I wasn't happy! My studio was divided into two large rooms. My show producers and my board operator were in the control room, and I was alone on the other side of the large soundproof glass window.

I was on the air when they walked in. I could tell by her body language that she was uncomfortable as she waved at me from the other side of the glass. Once my talk break was over, we went into a six-minute commercial break. I gestured for my producers to bring her over to get situated in the chair in front of me for her interview. Bear in mind that we only had six minutes.

So, who do you think walks into my side of the studio as I'm frantically rushing to prep this woman? The husband! He was the plus one at the receptionist's desk, holding things up! The moment they walked into the studio, I could sense his insecurities. I tried to disguise my irritation as I stood up from my chair to shake his hand. I said hello to her as she was being rushed to set up across from me by my senior producer.

I was about to ask him to return to the other side of the glass until the interview was over when he suddenly plopped down into the chair next to her and made himself comfortable. At this point, it had become obvious to everyone that she was in a hostage situation. I mean that figuratively, of course, but it was clear that he wanted to be there to block whatever he thought was going down!

Only a minute was left before we were back on the air live. So, I said under my breath, "Fuck it!" And I focused on getting through the interview.

Needless to say, it didn't go well. She was awkward and not at all the bubbly and witty personality I had spoken to over the phone, and his energy was just controlling and weird. It took all the fun out of it. To this day, it was the strangest interview I've ever had.

Once it was over, she and I were able to get a couple of minutes alone while he was in the control room, flirting with one of my producers. She apologized profusely and said she hoped we could do it again. I lied and told her, "Sure, stay in touch!" And then I had my producer escort her and his crazy ass out of the building.

His behavior didn't only project insecurity but narcissism. I could only imagine how his anxiety must have been building up over that week as he listened to me promoting his wife and her book on the radio in Dallas and to the entire country.

And maybe he was insecure about her meeting me too. I know I'm no Denzel Washington, but I'm not bad on the eyes! All joking aside, I got the impression he was more concerned about his wife becoming successful than running off with me. Sometimes watching a woman's career take off can make a man more insecure than competing with another man. And if you add both of those elements, watch out! You can get full-blown crazy!

The extent of the damage to her career is something we'll never know since that opportunity was missed. But it did discourage me from producing more *Living Your Dream* features for authors! It's unfortunate how the dreams and aspirations of others can be destroyed by one person's act of insecurity and jealousy. They are truly dream killers!

There's a lesson in this story for those of you who are entrepreneurs: be mindful of the partners you choose. Being in a relationship with a person with a nine-to-five mentality is entirely different than having a partner who marches to the beat of their own drummer. That's not to say they can't co-exist, but sometimes your partner can't accept the old you because they don't see themselves in the future of the new you! One day you're with the love of your life, and the next thing you know, you're sleeping with the enemy!

■ ■ ■

The title of this chapter, Hike The Ball, was mostly inspired by whether women should trust men with their heart and their emotional wellness. Most women have the objective of loving and nurturing, but too many of them get taken advantage of because of the influence of Hollywood movies, fairytales, religion, and their upbringing. It's programmed into women at a very young age to see intoxicating love as the only real love. Stories of love create the belief that a hero will come riding in on a white horse to save the day.

In too many women's minds, the idea of a Prince Charming is real, or they believe the Lord will send them someone when it's their time. And once a woman experiences that euphoric love, whether it's triggered by physical attraction, sexual addiction, or because the conniving man caught her at a vulnerable time in her life, she's likely to hike the ball to him emotionally.

I wrote the following commentary some months ago to warn women to be careful of to whom they give their hearts.

Many women crave love, are programmed to love, and believe they are born to love! But there are men out there who will take advantage of that genuine yearning with no intention of loving you back. Read these words and share them with a woman who is determined to love, even when the man doesn't deserve her love.

■ ■ ■

As men, we know when a woman loves us and when she's vulnerable. We also know when she wants something we can't or won't give her, such as children, marriage, love, or monogamy.

It's the responsibility of a real man to respect his woman enough to let her go instead of taking advantage of her sexually, financially, and emotionally, knowing he will never reciprocate the love she is giving him.

And it is the responsibility of the women to love themselves enough to recognize these pretenders and stop wasting their bodies, love, and valuable time hoping their overwhelming love will transform them— because it won't!

— Michael Baisden

While some view religion as a way to salvation and live a better life, others use it as a prop to disguise their hypocrisy, cheating, and abuse.

Sadly, women fall prey to these church players, giving them more credit than they deserve simply because they attend church and recite scripture. They believe these men are better because they claim to be "God-fearing."

But are men truly God-fearing? Or are they men who fear women discovering the truth? And that is, a good man is defined by his actions and integrity, not by what he believes or whether or not he worships in church.

Don't ever forget that!

10

LYING ASS CHURCH MEN!

I've been very public about my issues with some of these crooked pastors, the corruptive power of mega-churches, hypocritical believers, and religion in general. But guess who has an even bigger issue with organized religion? Christians who take their belief seriously!

It's no wonder church attendance is down. People are beginning to open their eyes and see these so-called religious leaders for what they are: con men! And members of congregations are being called out for their "Do as I say, not as I do" attitudes. We all see these pastors engaging in sex with church members, misusing church funds, sexually abusing children, and endless scheming, jealousy, and backstabbing. I mean, how much hypocrisy can a person take?

It's time for society, and the world for that matter, to get real and state the obvious—people who attend church are no better than people who don't, nor should they be expected to be! It shouldn't matter what someone says their belief is or what church they attend. Ultimately, it's a person's behavior that matters.

I think most of us accept this as truth, especially when it comes to the conduct of most men. Whether they claim to believe in Christ, Mohammad, or some deity, we all know that men are, well, just men. I don't care if that man prays every day, quotes scripture, tithes, or speaks in tongues; he is just a man.

In fact, most women will tell you that churchmen are even worse! Personally, I don't attend church, so I can't tell you what goes on in these buildings. But most of the people I interact with in my personal life consider themselves to be Christians. Some of them are positive and charitable, and some of them are arrogant assholes. As I said, religion and belief are not factors in determining a person's character. At least, that's been my experience.

I posed this question to my social media followers, who have more experience than I do with dating churchmen. I asked them whether these men made better or worse partners. I'm sure these stories will sound very familiar to many of you.

Rhonda wrote:

A so-called minister got physically aggressive with me despite my repeated objections. Kept laughing and saying God told him to lay hands on me. I excused myself, saying I was going to the bathroom, and came back with my pistol and told him that God didn't tell me to kill him, but if he didn't leave right then, I would. Needless to say, we never spoke again.

■ ■ ■

Rhonda's story made me wonder, have churchmen just said, "Fuck it!" and are no longer trying to disguise their lack of compliance with whatever religion they're supposed to represent? And by churchmen, I mean pastors, deacons, reverends, bishops, cardinals, and popes. Have they accepted that people know they're full of shit and don't care how they're perceived, or they've become unconscious of it?

Now bear in mind that I'm only referring to the ones acting out! Plenty of people take their relationship with God seriously, but I think we'd all have to agree they're in the minority!

But getting back to Rhonda's comment, when you have pastors openly and nonchalantly forcing themselves on female members, it's not an isolated incident—it's a common practice.

Hundreds of women posted a comment under the banner about Lying Ass Churchmen, and hundreds of them liked Rhonda's comment. Here are some other comments.

Shauna wrote:
Had a patient confide to me that her ex-husband who was a pastor slept with multiple women in her own home.

Bianca wrote:
An associate minister told me that 'the Lord said I was going to be his wife' ... though he was already married. False prophet!

Carla wrote:
My first husband was a minister and when I met him, he came on very strong and persistent, and he wasn't just handing out communion, nor did we miss any fellowship. After he passed away, I became an ordained minister... which was short lived.

Pastors, ministers, and church clergy are men and women first, far from perfect but should be above reproach as men and women. They should lead by example in how not to defile the temple of God and not give in to the temptations of the flesh.

I could write a book about "Churchmen." My experiences are exhaustive after being in the Church for several years. I'm done extensive studying on Bible history and researched several books on history, and my findings have been very eye-opening to hidden truths behind religion and many lies that we have adopted as truth. All I can say is to get your facts straight.

■ ■ ■

I agree with Carla; people need to do their own research to understand how to separate parables from actual history as well as educate themselves about human nature. Believing in something, no matter how strong that belief is, will not take away a personal sexual desire or their need for attention, nor will it magically transform a person's true character. In fact, the church is the perfect hunting ground for men to prey on women struggling with a multitude of issues, whether it's sexual abuse, low self-esteem, or abandonment issues.

I'm not knocking churchmen for their attraction to women

or being flirtatious; as I said, that's a normal human impulse. I'm putting them on blast for pretending to be better men when they're not! When it's all said and done, a man's integrity is the only quality that matters. That cannot and should not be minimized. A man's word is as basic as it gets in defining him as "Good!" So, if he doesn't measure up to that standard, then everything else he claims to represent is a running game and bullshit!

A popular biblical scripture speaks to how we should vet those who seek to influence and lead men. It's a verse from the book of Matthew 7:16–20 that reads:

You will know them by their fruits. Grapes are not gathered from thorn bushes, nor figs from thistles, are they? Even so, every good tree bears good fruit; but the bad tree bears bad fruit. A good tree cannot produce bad fruit, nor can a bad tree produce good fruit. Every tree that does not bear good fruit is cut down and thrown into the fire. So then, you will know them by their fruits. Judge a fruit by its tree.

Well, I've got my axe out, and I'm ready to chop down some of these lying ass men (trees) who are bearing bad fruit. I'm swinging away in this book and on my social media page, yelling, "TIMBER!"

Just as it's important to understand your cultural history, it's important to understand biblical history so that you don't have to rely on the word of others. Think for yourself, and make up your own mind about how to apply the religious text. This is why I promote educating yourself by reading history books, watching reputable academic lectures, and traveling to places like Egypt, Ghana, Paris, South Africa, and Greece. See the world, learn about different cultures, and above all else, question everything!

Religion is very influential. It only makes sense to learn the origins of something that's such a huge part of our lives, whether it's being used for good or if it's being used to exploit. You should better understand where it comes from and how it is fundamentally being used to impact your community, your race, and the world.

Then it's up to you to decide if you want to continue to literally believe in God, Jesus, Allah, Muhammad, Krishna, etc. All I'm saying is, do your homework!

■ ■ ■

There's nothing more low-down than a man who takes advantage of women seeking salvation or trying to heal from trauma by exploiting their vulnerabilities and ignorance of biblical scripture. Churchmen, and male church leaders, are notorious for Bible-whipping women with verses to keep them in place while simultaneously flipping scriptures to justify being greedy, lying, molesting children, and abusing women in the congregations.

The most popular of all time is Matthew 26:41. It reads: *Watch and pray so that you will not fall into temptation. The spirit is willing, but the flesh is weak.*

I assure you this verse wasn't meant to be a tool for trifling men to scapegoat their raggedy undisciplined behavior. Every time they get busted, they deny and deflect. When faced with irrefutable evidence and backed into a corner, they play their best card. The excuse usually begins with the words, "But Jesus said...."

Women, you should especially beware! Men often use these religious institutions as a sexual stalking ground. They prey on women serious about growing spiritually and who they know take the Bible literally. The grooming begins with directing them to scriptures to pressure them into submission— submission to God, submission to the church leaders, and submission to churchmen. Sure, there are many female pastors nowadays, and that's a good thing, but regardless of who's in charge, the Bible verses don't change. The manipulation and lying continue, and the games go on! Here are more verses that should make any intelligent woman ask, "Is this God or man?"

But if this thing be true, and the tokens of virginity be not found for the damsel: Then they shall bring out the damsel to the door of her father's house, and the men of her city shall stone her with stones that she die." — **Deuteronomy 22:20–21**

"I do not permit a woman to teach or to exercise authority over a man; rather, she is to remain quiet." — **Timothy 2:12**

"And everything on which she lies during her menstrual impurity shall be unclean. Everything also on which she sits shall be unclean." — **Leviticus 15:20**

"Wives, submit to your husbands as to the Lord." — **Ephesians 5:22**

"Let your women keep silence in the churches: for it is not permitted unto them to speak; but they are commanded to be under obedience as also saith the law. And if they will learn anything, let them ask their husbands at home: for it is a shame for women to speak in the church." —
1 Corinthians 14:34-35

■ ■ ■

You're all welcome to believe these are words inspired by a God, or you can conclude that these words were written by men who lived in a time when women had no voice, freedom, rights, and education.

Whatever you choose to believe religious text literally, please make sure it's based on your own in-depth research. Not what the pastor said, not what your husband or boyfriend feeds you, and not what your parents raised you to believe. After all, they're only teaching you what their parents taught them. But is that the whole story?

My philosophy has always been to question everything and to judge people based on their conduct, not what they say they believe! A person's belief or religion doesn't tell me anything about who they are, but their actions tell me everything! Look at the statistics; organized religion is dying while spirituality is growing. Young people, especially, are opening their eyes and challenging tradition. They see the hypocrisy, as we all do, and are saying "No, thank you" to church service, Sunday school, and old-fashioned rules that restrict them from being who they are. Little by little, the blinds are being taken off. And now, there's an outright exodus away from these Pimps In The Pulpit!

Michelle wrote:

When I moved to Georgia and the "popular" church wanted to see my W-2 to attend. Oh, and the seats up front were for the celebrities.

Tia Hilton wrote:

Preachers begging everyone to give give give. When the minister said, "turn to your neighbor and ask them to borrow $50 so you can put it in the basket", I took my babies and left.

Janel wrote:

I left because what I knew and felt did not match up with what I was being taught. I took African and African American studies as a second major in college. Once you know, you can't undo the knowledge. I tried to still go because my parents are both ministers. But after a while, it became humorous to go knowing what I know.

■ ■ ■

For goodness's sake, ladies, stop allowing these men to exploit you just because they claim to be a Christian, a Muslim, a Jew, a Hindu, or whatever! There are no statistics I'm aware of that prove that churchmen are more honest, more likely to pay their child support, and better fathers or partners. There's no proof that these men are more reliable or less likely to abuse their partners. In fact, some people say it's just the opposite—that they're worse!

But if you're determined to find a "God-fearing" man, then take my advice, slow your roll, and get to know him before you dive in emotionally—and before you let him dive into you. And while you're getting to know him, observe him. Pay close attention to see if he demonstrates how his beliefs manifest positive things in his life and contribute to his becoming a better person.

Personally, I think women should be wary of choosing a partner who believes they NEED God or a religious book to do the right thing. I'm not knocking the good work that some religious institutions and pastors do, but to say that those people would not perform those same duties without belonging to a religion or believing in God is contradictory to what it means to be an authentically good person.

When a good man gives his word to do something or tells you, "This is who I am," he means it because he's standing on his principles and good character, period! People with bad intentions rarely ever change into people with good intentions, at least not because of church attendance. Just as people who are fair and charitable. They don't do it for any reason except they hope people will be fair and charitable to them when they need help! And by the way, being kind and helping people feels good!

I think women should beware of any man who implies or admits he only does the right thing out of fear of punishment from hell or because he expects a reward from above. People who are good are not good because they believe they're being watched. They're good because that's who they are. Just as the liar continues to lie because that is who he is.

Every Sunday, these suited-down hypocrites attend services while gripping their Bibles as they file down the aisles. Their eyes constantly probe the room, searching for the attractive new female members or "fresh meat." For the horny arrogant men on the deacon board and the married and single cheating men in the congregation, it's a race to see who will be the first to "lay hands" on her.

I can only deduct from the behavior of these men that they're either pretending to believe in and fear God, they believe but are too trifling to care, or they're too weak to change! Either way, they're no better than a man who has never stepped foot in a church!

HAVING GREAT SEX
IS IMPORTANT!

Great sex feels good and is a gauge of how healthy your relationship is. Touching, kissing, and penetration reveals more than you think. Having great sex means the business of the relationship is being handled, and trust is strong. It's also a sign the passion is still there.

But when your sex life starts to decline, all kinds of problem begin to surface. So, when I hear people say, "Sex isn't important," I think to myself, You're just not doing it right!

11

STOP LYING ABOUT NOT WANTING GREAT SEX

If sex isn't important to you, skip this chapter. As a matter of fact, skip this entire book! As far as I'm concerned, sex is everything! Sexual energy is healing energy! Sexual energy is a source of happiness and self-confidence! And having healthy attitudes about sex is key to creating and maintaining deep bonds in relationships.

When the sex stops, the interest fades. The result is a cascade of issues from diminished sexual attraction to heightened irritation where everything your partner does annoys the hell out of you. When they laugh out loud, you roll your eyes. Their snoring makes you cringe when it has never bothered you before. Even the sound of them chewing food can set you off! That's because when you're having great sex, your partner's shortcomings seem, well, short and unimportant. But once that tranquilizer is taken away, every incompatible trait and every trivial issue becomes a trigger!

It's foolish for couples not to expect their relationship to change dramatically once the sex gradually or abruptly falls off! Some couples don't even acknowledge the decline because they focus on their careers and the children. Sometimes, using both is a distraction to avoid addressing the issue. But the moment they experience an awkward sexual moment or when the subject of sex is brought up in the company of friends who are having great sex, they face the reality of becoming what they've always dreaded; the sexless couple.

I used to wonder why so many people I encountered always seemed so cranky while I was always happy. Well, it's simple; they weren't having great sex, and I was, plenty of it! I read an article on CNN Health that said Americans are at a 30-yr low for sex. And half of Americans don't even have it once a month.

The New York Times reported that since 1973, men have lost 50% of their testosterone at a rate of 1% yearly, along with diminishing sperm count. It's no wonder many women who want children struggle to become pregnant. It's not due to bad eggs but lazy sperm. And a report on sex by The Daily Caller says that 26% of Americans, i.e., 1 in 4, haven't had sex in the last year! And we wonder why the world is so screwed up and tight-assed! We need more sex, dammit!

Just think about all the issues created because of the lack of great sex in the world: people are less patient and more irritable, everyone is tired because they're not getting a good night's sleep, and our skin just doesn't have that glow to it. People not having sex are missing out on what I like to call The Fresh Fuck Look!

Ladies, do you ever notice how when you're in a good

relationship and having great sex, people are drawn to you? Perfect strangers walk up to you out of nowhere, saying things like, "Excuse me, I just wanted to pay you a compliment. You look amazing! You're really glowing!" You blush and reply, "Why, thank you!" But what you're really thinking at that moment is, I'm glowing because my man blew my back out last night—and this morning!

So, ladies, start weaning yourself off anti-depressants today and consider using less coconut oil you have stocked in your medicine cabinet. All you need to relieve your anxiety and make your skin shine is a good man and some good dick! No more negative side effects from Prozac, like headaches, nausea, and weight gain. Whereas the side effects of great sex are something to look forward to, such as relaxation, the sun seeming to shine brighter, and the best sleep ever because great sex will knock your ass out!

So, you may be asking, "Michael, where do women find these good men who provide all this great sex?" Well, ladies, they're all around you; the guy delivering packages, the man at the grocery stores who is checking you out, and your local cigar bars where there are many single men.

But here's where I think women are creating limitations and restrictions. They complain that some men are too arrogant, but men who are the best lovers are typically the most confident. Some women would even go so far as to call them overconfident or cocky. But he's cocky because he knows he has a good cock!

Stay with me, ladies. I'll be brief, but this is important!

There's a new term for assertive men who tell women straight up, "I just want sex!" And maybe he's married, and he's straight up about that too, and he still tells you, "I just want sex!" Today, they label these men as "toxic." I believe this term has been misused to describe men who won't do what women want them to do. Whether he's a married cheater or in an open relationship, the point is, if he's being honest about wanting sex while having other partners, how is that toxic? It's wrong, of course, but toxic? Come on, ladies!

When did this stop being attractive and become "toxic"? The majority of women reading this have dealt with a married man or a man who was involved with other women, but he didn't become "toxic" until she didn't get what she expected out of it. If we're keeping it real, many women are attracted to aggressive, confident, accomplished, and unavailable men. The ones available are boring, and women love a challenge.

They don't want an emotionally vulnerable man they can curl up with while watching romantic comedies. They want a stud that's going to come by and blow her back out, ask you to fix him a sandwich afterward, and then go another round before he rolls out at 11 p.m. so he can get back to his other woman and some rest before work.

Women who are serious about wanting a man who will provide consistently great sex, has swag, and won't bug the shit out of her by blowing up her phone every day must accept that he might be considered a little toxic or, a term I prefer to use, "He's untamable!" And untamable men will never conform to women's ideal of being sensitive like Russel Wilson, engaging like Don Lemon, and insightful like Deepak Chopra. They are interesting because they are not tamable, and women who are honest with themselves know that to be true. So, either stop lying about not liking toxic men or stop calling them toxic!

But keep in mind that the so-called toxic man will kill bugs, mow the lawn, and protect you from real assholes. And yes, he may be a little toxic, but he brings that Big Dick energy! And women love that! Hell, they need it!

Now, I know some of the ladies reading this have their faces turned up, saying, "Fuck men, I have my rose!" To that, I say, "Good for you. May you and your rose live happily ever after." But for those women who don't use toys or who eventually want to be held, to be loved, and to be asked, "Whose Pussy is this?" at some point, you'll have to learn to deal with us and settle for a little toxicity to get to the other parts of us that are useful—even if only for one night!

■ ■ ■

To be fair, the biggest challenge to women regarding sex isn't tolerating untamed or toxic men. The real elephant in the room is men's health—or a lack of it. The sad truth is too many men are coming up short in the bedroom because they're not taking care of themselves. Amongst the biggest lies men tell themselves is that having high blood pressure, being overweight, and taking a bunch of prescription medications don't matter. Well, it does!

And once your Johnson stops working, it won't matter how much money you have, how good you look, or how much pussy you eat; a woman is never happy when her man won't address the root of the problem. As a man who had to address his sexual issues related to diabetes, I'm speaking from experience when I warn men to confront these issues head-on before they cascade into a multitude of mental, egotistical, and sexual issues.

Women are finally opening up to enjoying sex. And as they

age, their sexual desires increase, while too many men find themselves in sexual decline, unable to satisfy their partners. When I talk about being unable, I'm referring to issues such as high blood pressure, diabetes, obesity, and poor diets, to name a few. These conditions are preventable with a rigorous exercise regimen and healthy eating.

You would think that a man's ego alone would be enough to inspire him to keep up with his health, but some men just won't put in the effort and create a society of sexually frustrated women who are just reaching their peak! This leaves women who are 'ready' with fewer options or having to settle for sexually inadequate companions. And that's sad and unfair!

Can you imagine waiting your entire life to release the freak only to reach your 40s and 50s to discover there's no one to release the freak with? The children are finally out of the house, you're financially stable, eating healthier and working out, and sexually you're ready to rumble! Hell, the sex drive of some of these women is so strong it's the men who might get their backs blown out!

I have several attractive female friends over 50 who constantly complain they can't find an older gentleman with whom they have things in common. And even when they connect with one, he typically has sexual issues. So, instead of dating someone in their age group, which they prefer, many of them are entertaining younger men. These younger men may not have the mannerisms my friends prefer, but they do match their sexual energy, and they're socially active. Too many men over fifty are comfortable just lying around the house watching TV. If a woman is lucky, she might get sex once a week when she really wants to get tossed every night!

But here's where the news gets even worse for women. Not only do men over 50 struggle with erectile dysfunction, but men under 40 are also having issues. Women are experiencing a tremendous amount of anxiety, wondering if they'll ever find a compatible sex partner. Forget about expecting someone to be husband or boyfriend material. Women can't even get laid properly!

But don't take my word for it. Read what women had to say when I posted about the issue of Erectile Dysfunction on my Facebook Page. I could have written a book with the number of posted comments. Here are a few of the more interesting ones.

Cynthia wrote:

Sad to say my husband was in denial! I was willing to compromise but you can't be in this alone. So, six months ago I walked away from 28 years of marriage.

Anna wrote:

It is a real issue and women should work with their partner. A guy can use his fingers and tongue and we live in a time where sexual toys available. As a couple deal with the issue together...The experience can be quite satisfying!

Synnesterra wrote:

ED can cause you to go from being in a relationship to having a roommate. I dated someone who had issues and I tried be supportive, suggesting that he make changes to his diet, exercise a little more, and go see a doctor. He was not receptive to that or to any alternatives of intimacy. It went on until we drifted apart.

Mary wrote:
The intimacy is no longer there causing anxiety and frustration within the relationship. Tension arises causing arguments rather than conversation. It's devastating for the man and he usually shuts down with denial vs understanding the older you get you begin having problems in this area. Exercise and eating healthy is the key.

Takesha wrote:
It can be very problematic if the two aren't able to communicate and discuss alternate ways of intimacy. Or it can be tolerable if both parties are willing to compromise. If not, it becomes a major problem and the relationship will fail. The man feeling inadequate and insecure and refuses to disclose and talk about his issue could result with the woman feeling unattractive and undesirable.

David wrote:
I think it is incumbent upon the man being upfront with his "meat". E.D is often a sign of other physical problems related to diabetes, high blood pressure, or both. Sometimes, anti-depressants can cause ED. Maybe the medication should be switched up. If a man truly cares about his partner, he's going to address his issues. If a woman truly loves her partner, she's going to support him. If it is an issue that cannot be resolved through medication or surgery, then the two of them can still find a way to be sexually intimate and experience pleasure. If not, then they should part ways.

Grace wrote:

You should get your A1C checked as E.D. is a condition that some men with diabetes suffer from. This was the case with my ex-husband. I helped him from the beginning (before marriage) to get that sugar under control and he started taking a pill for it. When you love someone, truly love someone, you will support them. Now, if he doesn't want to get the help that can enhance a better quality of life for himself then maybe you should move on. My opinion from my own experience.

James wrote:

Maybe he can't get it up because he's no longer stimulated by his partner. I know plenty of men who could not get aroused due to having a partner who was boring in bed. Over time women need to spice things up then maybe the man could get it up! Try some new tricks, ladies, suck his balls, wear something sexy, swing on a pole, and for God's sake, take that damn mummy wrap off your head! That will cause a man to go limp faster than anything!

Liz wrote:

James, it's comments like yours that are contributing to men not getting the help they need. Not being aroused because a woman is wearing a head wrap to bed has nothing to do with E.D. But instead of men like you addressing their health issues they deflect and start blaming the woman. Well, that's a bunch of B.S.! It's also childish and damaging to couples who are looking for real answers.

*And BTW, women get turned off sexually with a lot of sh*t
you men do...and by what you don't do. If you want us to
be wet and ready try taking out the f***king garbage without
constantly being asked. Or washing your ass so we don't
have to see the skit marks in your draws.*

*And maybe if you men led properly we would put in the extra
effort to dress sexy, but who has time when you have to play
your role and his. Sorry I got off topic but this deflecting
instead of confronting the problem sets me off!*

■ ■ ■

So, this is where we are in society today. Millions of single
and married women are adamant about loving sex, wanting
sex, needing sex, and don't necessarily need a commitment
to have sex. What's the world coming to when women are
ready to fuck but can't find men who are fuckworthy? Or
can't fuckin' keep up!

And while we're on the subject, let me challenge the
men who are reading this book to not only improve their
sexual health but to open their minds. Besides, the issue of
not being able to maintain an erection is the issue of men
not allowing women to be their true sexual selves without
being judged.

I don't mean to beat a dead horse, but women have a
lot of obstacles when it comes to expressing themselves
sexually. There's not a man alive who would trade places
with a woman in this dating environment, especially Black
men! Not only is the ratio of available women to men 20 to
1, but the level of sexual close-mindedness of Black men is
mind-blowing!

Women must not only find a partner who is transparent, health conscious, consistent, and interested in actively courting her, but they also must find one who isn't insecure about his own sexuality or theirs. We live in a time where women are masturbating more than ever, exploring same-sex relationships, experimenting with kinks, and singing about having WAP (Wet-Ass Pussies).

Men better get their act together and let go of their traditional ideas about sex and relationships because women are already in a new space mentally and sexually. Women want to try new things, explore different relationship dynamics, and step outside the box of what they've been told "good girls" don't do. The secret is out that a lot of women love being choked, enjoy dirty talk, wear collars, use sex toys, have experimented with bisexuality, fantasize as men do about having threesomes, and want a partner who is turned on by them squirting uncontrollably on the bed and on him.

As I said, women are ready to take their sexuality to the next level! Hell, they've been ready for a while. They just didn't have a man open-minded enough to be a nasty girl with. In my opinion, men are standing in the way of the next sexual revolution. The reality is the kink train has already left the station—men just haven't figured it out yet!

So, what is a freak? Well, what's freaky to me might be basic to someone else—it's subjective. But to me, being a freak means you're sexually adventurous and rarely say "no" to trying something new.

The term "freak" identifies a person who is in touch with their sexuality and who marches to the beat of their own sensual drum. Labels don't work for them!

In short, to me—being a freak means you're open-minded, uninhibited, and free! So, here's a shout-out to all the freaks like me!

— Michael Baisden

12

RELEASE THE FREAK!
STOP LYING ABOUT NOT BEING KINKY

So, why are people afraid to release their inner freak? Simple, it's the fear of being judged. Most people cannot stand the idea of being looked at differently by those close to them. Or they don't want to risk a potential partner not viewing them as a "good catch" because of their sexual appetite. Women are worried they'll be called whores for desiring multiple partners, and men are petrified of being labeled as gay if they admit to enjoying a woman pegging them or even licking their ass.

These close-minded and homophobic attitudes are keeping us in the dark about our true sexual identity while giving power to those who don't have the guts to explore their own sexuality. The time has come to take the stage back from these cowards and put it in the hands of courageous people who understand that our freaky nature, nastiness, and kinks are a part of who we are—and it's nothing to be ashamed of!

But where do these restrictive attitudes come from? The straightforward answer is culture and religion. I define culture as the values and customs we are exposed to by our society and communities and the standards and lessons taught to us by our families.

If you were raised in a culture and a family with certain beliefs about sex and sexuality, you probably would share those same attitudes. As an African American male raised on the South Side of Chicago, I never received a real education about sex, and neither did most of the Black people I grew up with. Most of our parents didn't talk openly about sex, and the school systems didn't have anything to offer that was relatable.

And as far as society is concerned, everybody knows America is a hypocritical and secrecy society when it comes to discussing sex, so there was nothing to learn there—except maybe how to hide your *Playboy* and *Hustler* magazines under your mattress.

Releasing the freak is hard almost anywhere in the world except for a few countries like Thailand, Netherlands, Denmark, Bangladesh, and cities in the U.S. such as Los Angeles, San Francisco, and Atlanta. Most of the world is still living in denial about prostitution, alternative lifestyles, and the growing number of people into kink!

It's hard to believe that in 2023, people are still being taught that sex is meant only for marriage, women's pleasure is secondary to the man's, and only "good girls" or virgin-like women will attract a good man. That's such bullshit! And you have culture to blame for most of this old-fashioned thinking.

While writing this chapter, I took a break to visit my favorite marijuana dispensary. I struck up a conversation with my Uber driver, who was from India. He shared with me that his two grown sons, 24 and 28 years old, still lived with him. The older son was about to get married, and he offered to let them both stay at the family home with him and his wife. The son declined, preferring to get a place on his own. The point of that story is that it's not an American custom. In this country, once you decide to get married, you've got to go! In fact, leave the day after you turn 18 if possible.

But the main point of this story is what he shared next. The younger son was having a hard time connecting with a partner to marry, so the father said, "If he doesn't find someone soon, my wife and I will choose someone for him!" In my mind, I'm thinking, Did he just say that? But I quickly compose myself, understanding that this is still normal for some cultures. And it stands to reason that many sexual acts are also viewed as out of bounds until marriage and possibly not allowed altogether!

What is not normal or sustainable is people suppressing their true sexuality. And you hear this rebellion being reflected more and more in today's music. The younger generation is leading the way. And many older men and women decide to come out of the closet with their kinks and alternative lifestyles. People don't realize the freak was released decades ago, and it's just starting to bubble to the surface. In my opinion, it's about damn time!

Why shouldn't a woman be comfortable saying "I want a man with a big dick?" Or "I like to watch my man have sex with another woman?" Or "I like to have him watch me have sex with another man?" If that's her preference, then she should speak up. As the saying goes, "The squeaky wheel gets the grease!"

And why should a man have to hide his kink of enjoying being pegged by his woman or being peed on? Or maybe it turns him on to be dominated? My motto is, "If you like it, I love it!" Besides, people are doing it anyway! And what's so hilarious is that some of the biggest freaks are in the most conservative states. You think California is freaky? Shit! The conservative red state of Texas is freak-central! There are Swingers and Adult Only clubs everywhere, Kink groups, and a large bisexual and poly community in Houston. You name it; they got it in Texas. And wouldn't you know, Texas just happens to be one of the most religious states in the country. I love me some Bible belt freaks!

This brings me to the second major factor in what's stifling freedom of sexual expression; the Holy Bible! Inspired or invented by men, (you decide) interpreted by men, edited by men, and controlled by men. These ancient storytellers didn't know the world was round, why volcanos erupted, what bacteria was, approved of slavery, and treated women as property whose sole purpose on Earth was to procreate and serve men!

To be fair in my critique, the Koran, Tora, or any other ancient religious book that people take literally is also demeaning to women. Just read some of these biblical passages, and you decide if these are God's words or the words of men trying to keep a handle on women's bodies.

Let marriage be held in honor among all, and let the marriage bed be undefiled, for God will judge the sexually immoral and adulterous. — **Hebrews 13:4**

For this is the will of God, your sanctification: that you abstain from sexual immorality; that each one of you know how to control his own body in holiness and honor, not in the passion of lust like the Gentiles who do not know God. — **1 Thessalonians 4:3-5**

Flee from sexual immorality. Every other sin a person commits is outside the body, but the sexually immoral person sins against his own body. Or do you not know that your body is a temple of the Holy Spirit within you, whom you have from God? You are not your own, for you were bought with a price. So glorify God in your body. — **1 Corinthians 6:18-20**

To the unmarried and the widows, I say that it is good for them to remain single as I am. But if they cannot exercise self-control, they should marry. For it is better to marry than to burn — **1 Corinthians 7:8-9**

"If a man seduces a virgin who is not betrothed and lies with her, he shall give the bride-price for her and make her his wife. If her father utterly refuses to give her to him, he shall pay money equal to the bride-price for virgins. — **Exodus 22:16-17**

Or do you not know that the unrighteous will not inherit the kingdom of God? Do not be deceived: neither the sexually immoral, nor idolaters, nor adulterers, nor men who practice homosexuality, nor thieves, nor the greedy, nor drunkards, nor revilers, nor swindlers will inherit the kingdom of God. — **1 Corinthians 6:9-10**

But I say to you that everyone who looks at a woman with lustful intent has already committed adultery with her in his heart. — **Matthew 5:28**

■ ■ ■

Can you imagine being indoctrinated with this kind of language as a child and then having it reinforced by telling you these are God's words? It's no wonder people are so fucked up! No disrespect to my believers, but this doesn't sound like a God speaking but rather a bunch of controlling, manipulating, and insecure men. If a man said those words in plain English to the average twenty-two-year-old today, he would be told to go to hell! (pun intended)

Look, you can believe in a higher power and gain inspiration from ancient texts without buying into literal interpretations. Too many people have been emotionally scarred, sexually assaulted, and had their sexuality suppressed by these Bible-thumping men who claim to be speaking for God. Meanwhile, these holier-than-thou churchmen run wild and unprotected through the congregation!

We're all sexual beings—by design, whether you believe that's God's design or evolutions—and horny beings. The sooner we accept that, the sooner we can learn what stimulates us and pursue our nastiness, freakiness, and kinks without being subjected to all fear-mongering and institutionalized guilt. I want people to feel free to be themselves. Of course, I want them to be responsible, but that should go without saying. Just because you're a freak, nasty, or kinky doesn't mean you're reckless.

Again, that's the label people try to put on you when they're too afraid to be their true sexual selves. People get offended when you're not ashamed of things they find shameful. They resent you for not caring what people think. And they hate you because you're free and they're not! Never forget that!

I digressed. Let's get back into the kinky stuff!

■ ■ ■

In 2022, I created a group on Facebook called The Transparency Tribe. The inspiration for this group was to separate my "open-minded" followers from my more conservative ones. Once we reached 80,000 members, I made the group private.

And boy, let me tell you, once the public could no longer see what was going on inside the group, the freaks came out! I would never have imagined so many "normal looking" people with traditional nine-to-five jobs, as well as professionals, could be so damned nasty.

Topics I never in a million years would have posted on my Fan page were being posted, shared, and commented on by thousands of people all day, every day. Now, to be completely transparent, I wasn't familiar with many of the language people were using to describe their favorite kinks, so I had to do a little research to get up to speed.

For those of you who already know these terms, just move forward a few pages. But for those new to kink lingo, as I am, prepare yourself! I promise you this terminology will make you blush. I know I did!

KINK AND BDSM TERMINOLOGY

Abrasion Play – The use of something rough like sandpaper or a brush to provide stimulation

Aftercare Once – The scene is over, aftercare is the emotional and physical care that's administered, usually by a top that is used to prevent more intense emotional aftereffects. Proper aftercare may also be used to prevent a drop

Anal Training – Inserting progressively larger objects (usually butt plugs) to stretch the anal sphincter in preparation for anal activities

Animal Play – One partner, usually the submissive one, pretends to be an animal, often for the amusement, training, grooming, and affection of the Dominant

Bagging Suffocation – using a bag over someone's head as a turn on

Ball Busting – The act of inflicting intense pain to a man's genitals, either by kicking, punching, slapping, caning, etc., for his pleasure

BDSM Bondage Discipline Sadism Masochism –
A blanket term used to describe a sexual practice that involves the use of physical control, psychological power, or pain. It typically includes the components of bondage and discipline, domination and submission, or sadism or masochism

Bondage Acts – Involving the physical restraint of a partner

Brat – A submissive who enjoys playful banter with a dominant partner

Breath Play – Controlling and limiting the breathing of another person in a given scene (i.e., choking or asphyxiation)

Breeding – This usually means having unprotected sex to ejaculate. Most commonly refers to a fantasy where women are used solely for impregnation

Bunny – Primarily someone who bottoms in a rope scene

Camming sex – Via the internet with the use of webcams to view either or both directions

Cane – A thin rod used for striking, commonly made of hardwood bamboo or acrylic

Cat O'Nine Tails – Whip with nine tails or lashes

Chastity – A form of erotic sexual denial or orgasm denial where a person is prevented access to or stimulation of their genitals, sometimes by the use of a chastity belt

Cock Milking – The practice of forcing a male to discharge semen through the penis through prostrate massage without experiencing a pleasurable orgasm

Collar – A symbol used to represent a submissive or slave is owned. It can be an actual collar but can also be an anklet, bracelet, or anything the couple decides on

Dom – A dominant who is male

Dominatrix – A woman who is dominant, who can be a professional for pay, or may live the lifestyle, or engage in BDSM activities

Edging – Bringing someone close to the edge of having an orgasm and then denying the payoff

Electro Kink – Play that involves electrically-charged objects such as violet wants, stun guns, cattle prods

Fetish – An obsession with a specific experience, body part, or object that becomes one of sexual association

Fire and Ice Play – Alternating between hot candle wax and ice or ice water

Forced Orgasm – An orgasm that is induced on a person against their will

Gag – Any device or object placed in the mouth to prevent speech or loud noises. It can be used as a form of control or punishment

Glory Hole – A hole cut into a wall or partition used to perform anonymous sex acts, often in public settings such as bathrooms

Hair Bondage – Technique where the hair is secured in a way as to limit the mobility of the head or upper body

Hard Limits – An activity or sexual act that is off-limits, non-negotiable

Hedonistic – Pursuit of the pleasures

Horse – A piece of bondage furniture consisting of a plank supported by two legs on each end where a person may be bent or tied over to be flogged or spanked

Humiliation – This involves a sub agreeing to demeaning situations meant to demean and embarrass the sub by their Dom/Domme. It is often intentionally intensified through public acts

Impact Play – A type of BDSM play involving one person striking another. This can be done with whips, canes, paddles, a hand, a flogger, a riding crop, or other instruments

Master – The person who has control over a slave in a consensual master-slave relationship

Masochist – A person who likes or becomes sexually gratified by their own pain or humiliation

Munch – An informal meeting or party of new and active members, often at a public place, where people interested in BDSM can mingle and socialize

Painslut – A masochist who enjoys a strong degree of pain

Pansexual – Someone who is attracted to people regardless of their gender

Pearl Necklace – When a man ejaculates onto a neck

Pegging – Most common act of a female using a strap-on to penetrate a male anally

Queening – Sitting on another's face often to allow or force oral-genital/oral-anal contact

Rimming – Licking or inserting the tongue into another's anus

Role Play – A scene in which one or more participants assume a role

Sadism and Masochism – Sexual pleasure that involves inflicting pain or humiliation for pleasure or sexual gratification

Safe Word – A word or phrase used to slow down or stop a scene

Slave – A person who gives up control of one or more parts of their life to a master

Snowballing – Transferring semen from one mouth to another through kissing

Vanilla – A blanket term used for anything conventional; the opposite of kink

Voyeurism – Deriving sexual pleasure from watching others, usually without their knowledge

Wax Play – When the top drips hot wax onto the bottom

■ ■ ■

That's a lot going on, right? If your reaction was anything like mine after reading all this, you probably feel like you're the one who's Vanilla! I haven't done a fraction of those things, but they gave me some ideas I'd like to try. And I know some of you freaks like me were thinking the same thing.

Just make sure you have consent from your partners. Don't just come home one day and start choking your woman in bed and end up getting the shit slapped out of you and then turn around and blame me, talking about, "I read about it in Michael Baisden's book, and he said it would turn you on!" As I said, make sure you have consent—and a safe word!

When it comes to being freaky, the most important element is trust. In the case of a woman revealing their freaky side to her man, she must be careful not to allow the man to respond by becoming hypersexual. Instead of reaping the benefits of having a freaky woman, some men subconsciously begin to see their partner purely as a sex object and begin detaching from them emotionally. Men need to understand that a woman might reveal that she's into other women or other kinky stuff, but she still needs to be loved and handled affectionately and with respect. Without trust, no woman will be her true self and allow herself to explore.

And the same can be said for a man who's kinky. He needs to trust that his woman won't lose respect for him or accuse him of being gay or weak just because he enjoys anal play or is down with a threesome with his woman and another man. That's not being gay. It's a sign of a mature man who's confident he's holding it down! He's secure enough to allow his woman to release her inner freak and explore her fantasies, which is more than can be said of most men who only want threesomes of them and two women—and that's not fair!

The ability to be fair-minded and trustworthy is essential in reaching your freak potential. And it was my reputation as a fair and trustworthy person that allowed over 80,000 people to openly post about sex in an explicit way inside

The Transparency Tribe Group! They trusted that I would not share their comments without their consent, and most importantly, they knew I would never judge them. I try to remind them as often as possible never to entertain anyone who they don't trust to be themselves with. If you can't share your fantasies and trust that what you share together stays between you, walk away. In fact, don't walk—run!

It's a privilege to chat with mature adults who can say without hesitation, "I'm a squirter, and I'm looking for a partner who's into that! I think it's dope that women in the group who are newly single and in their fifties express that they're bored with men who want to make love all the time. "I want to fuck sometimes!" they say inside the group! One sixty-three-year-old woman commented on a post about dirty talk. "I enjoy being naughty in the bedroom, but he better not call me a bitch! I'm not into that dirty talk that disrespectful!". I guess she's classified as a freak apprentice. Here are some other comments I copied from the kink post in my group! If any of you who posted these are reading this book, I just want to say, "Y'all nasty! And I love you for it!"

Frank wrote:
My fantasy is to lay on bed with my dick facing the ceiling and 10 different ladies take turns and do reverse cowgirl on me for 30 seconds each, 'till I cum.

Tyrone wrote:
Sex with a midget or little person or however you say it.

Keda wrote:
I want to attend Hedonism in Jamaica!!!!!

Marquita wrote:
Role play, bondage, and using toys with my partner. I also love when he fucks my face.

Kevin wrote:
My list is extensive because I am a Daddy Dom but everything revolves around BDSM. Bandage, impact play, Sensor replay, Dominant/submissive, role playing. I have a very firm hand but a soft heart. Aftercare is extremely important.

Myron wrote:
Choke me, tie me, the more pain the more I respond. I don't bruise easy. Oh, and I love taking her water works in my mouth.

Chiriga wrote:
I own cuffs, a flogger, a paddle, arm spreader, ankle spreader, I haven't gotten into ropes, but I do like tape, blindfolds, and if anybody likes a lil hot wax play...just me...ok...lol

Stephanie wrote:
Anal and lowkey humiliation. I told a guy that once and he slapped TF out of me so that's why I say "lowkey" There's a way to do it darn it!

DON'T LIE TO ME

Kim wrote:
Wax play
Fire play
Flogging
Rope play
Knife play
Some bandage
Choking
Okay I'm going to stop lol

Kizza wrote:
I have sooooooooo many kinks and fetishes! Some are outright nasty and pleasurably disgusting lol Damn near anything and everything goes with me as long we're all of age adults with a highly sexually uninhibited open-mind and appetite for sexual exploring and adventure. My No's: no animals, no underage young girls, no corpses, no one on one sex play with another man without a woman servicing us both at same time.

Karen wrote:
I love the expression on a man's face when I look him dead in the eyes when I snatch his soul! Umm Umm Good!

Aundra wrote:
Choking (hands and gag ball), spanking, hair pulling, slapping, bondage, blindfold, following orders from my King as his sub.

Robin wrote:
Impact play, sensation play, ropes, wax play, role playing, edging, bondage, voyeurism, e-stim, dominant and submissive, scene play, BDSM...yes to the bd but no to the sm. lol

Autumn wrote:
Pain and passion and pleasure crops, whips, rope, belt, seeing, spanking, BDSM, choking, hot and cold stimulation, and rough house.

Carmen wrote:
CNC, rope play, choking, bondage, flogging, edging, milking, face sitting.

James wrote:
Role play, Mutual masturbation, toys, public sex, voyeurism, sex in front of others.

Leland wrote:
Wow! I had no idea how much stuff there was to do! And I was unaware of what was out there. People have really taken their sexuality to creative new heights.

■ ■ ■

I'm with you, Leland. I also had no idea there was this much "stuff" going on. I guess I've got to step my kink game up! It just goes to show you no matter how old you are and how much experience you think you have, there's always something new to explore. But for that to happen, the mental barriers must come down. The guilt-tripping has to stop.

Yes, some of those obstacles are religious-based, but I'm not going to let people off the hook that easy! While religion is a major factor in sexual repression, ultimately, we have a choice to remain ignorant and closed-minded.

In my opinion, it's not the fear of God that causes people to be judgmental and try to control their partner. It's fear that their partner may evolve into something they can't handle or control. There's only one word for a partner with that mind-set: "insecure," more specifically, "sexually insecure." And it must be confronted. No one should allow another person's lack of sexual confidence to keep them from living their best life and getting their freak on!

Now, turn the page, and let's get deep into the topic of sexual insecurities and sex toys, such as the infamous rose!

Men need to stop asking dumb questions like, "Where did you learn that from?"

Just relax and enjoy the ride!

— Anonymous

13

MY ROSE is NOT THE ENEMY!

PENIS SIZE, BODY COUNT, AND SEX TOYS

Insecurity can be a toxic and destabilizing force in a relationship. It creates feelings of jealousy and uneasiness, making you or your partner feel like you're not enough! The need to feel secure is essential to the success of any relationship, so it makes you wonder why people don't address sexual and self-esteem issues that could undermine their pursuit of a relationship from day one! Everyone is always parroting so-called relationship experts about how communication is key to a successful relationship, but most people are not transparent about their insecurities which could trigger them to act out.

These important issues must be put on the table before getting deeply involved. It makes no sense to wait until you've invested valuable time and become emotionally attached, only to discover serious issues that could cripple your relationship. The problem, of course, is getting that person to be honest about their insecurities, not only because they see their insecurities as embarrassing but potentially disqualifying. But it's your responsibility to ask the tough questions. After all, it's your valuable time that's being wasted if you don't speak up!

And if they choose to lie about it, at least you can confront them later by saying, "Look, I asked you at the beginning of this relationship if you had insecurities!" Personally, it's important to me, once their insecurities start revealing themselves, to be able to say to them, "I asked you, and you lied to me!" As opposed to sitting there looking stupid because I was too afraid to interview (vet) them properly.

The range of what causes a person to feel insecure is vast. It can be on issues relating to their height, weight, income, education, penis size, vaginal issues, body shape, skin tone, hair texture, or insecurity created by comparing themselves to others, which, in my opinion, is at the root of most insecurities.

We live in a culture of attention-seekers and showoffs! I called it the "Look at me—not at them!" mentality, and it's preventing us from finding acceptance within ourselves. And thanks to social media, the focus on "me-ism" has been elevated to a whole new level! People are bombarded daily with images that make them look at themselves more critically. It's nearly impossible not to see yourself as "less than" when you're constantly scrolling through pictures of women with perfect bodies and seemingly living the dream lifestyle. Men with bulging muscles are surrounded by gorgeous women posing in front of Rolls-Royces and Lamborghinis.

These extravagant images are powerful and influential, especially to our young people. It's no wonder so many of them suffer from low self-esteem. Recent studies have shown a dramatic increase in the number of teenagers who have attempted or committed suicide because they didn't feel like they measured up or fit in.

Back in the day, women only had to compete with images of models in magazines, whether it was the centerfold in the monthly edition of *Playboy* and *Hustler* or *The Jet's* beauty of the week. But today, the competition is worldwide and in vivid videos brought to you live and in living color courtesy of TikTok, Facebook, and Instagram.

Nearly everyone starts their day by waking up and checking their social media page. With the simple click of a button, you're treated to thousands of provocative videos featuring big asses, large breasts, and men in sweatpants showing off their dick imprints!

And here's where many men get messed up. They watch porn all day which, to some of them, represents what real women want and expect in the bedroom. Unless you're a mature man who understands how to separate entertainment from reality, you should immediately stop watching X-rated movies. Once those images of enormous penises, sex orgies, and women being flipped like hotcakes get branded into the mind of a young man, it's a wrap!

Mesmerized by how satisfied the women appear to be with all their moaning and screaming in ecstasy, the now delusional man starts taking mental notes on the technique the man in the movie is using, expecting to get the same response from a woman. He watches the movie, then pulls out his erect dick and looks at it, then back to the movie, then he looks back at his dick again, and that's when it hits him, "I don't have enough! I'm in trouble!" Or "I've got enough. Let me go to work!" Either way, he's wrong!

"Stop confusing entertainment for what women want in real life!" I've said to young men I've mentored. "That's not what women expect from you! That's what you expect from you!" I tell them.

It's a sexual fantasy, not reality, and men sometimes don't understand that it's all an act, especially all the fake moaning by women. Now, don't get me wrong, some ladies love a nice deep stroke of everything now and then, but they don't expect it. If they did require a man to have ten inches of Long Dong Silver, 95% of them would be hugely disappointed! Pun intended!

So, this is where sexual insecurity is born in the minds of many of our men. We, as men, have misguided ideas about how to handle a woman. We're obsessed with penis length and penis girth, and as a result, we have no real understanding of what stimulating a woman sexually really involves.

As for women, well, their insecurities have more to do with body types, such as concerns about height, weight, butt and breast size, and their overall body image. Many women also have insecurities about having vaginas that are too big or too tight. And a significant percentage of women feel insecure about not having enough sexual experience. They worry that the man they are attracted to won't choose them because they are not freaky enough or their oral skills aren't up to par. Put all that together, and what do you have? We have a bunch of horny adults with horrible communication skills and misinformation.

Well, take out your notepads, and let's break down these issues that can cause insecurities! Hopefully, by the time we're done with this chapter, you'll be able to get over yours— or at least be able to talk openly about them. Just like with Alcoholics Anonymous, the first step to recovery is admission. Now let's dive in!

■ ■ ■

PREMATURE EJACULATORS
a.k.a. Men With No Dick Control

Sexual insecurities can be caused by a man climaxing too fast during sex. No matter how big his penis is and how much the woman is attracted to him or cares for him, eventually, frustration will set in for her, and insecurity will creep into his mind. And what makes matters worse is when the man won't acknowledge that he's a fast cummer! I'm not sure that's a technical term for it, but let's go with it!

How a man wouldn't know that he's ejaculating too fast is beyond me, but obviously, it's happening. You would think that a grown man would have enough experience, or at least care enough to make sure his woman is properly "warmed up" before he selfishly climaxes. Because being selfish is what it boils down to in most cases, the man simply not giving a damn about the woman's needs being met.

I posed this issue to my followers on my social media pages. I asked them to measure on a scale of one to ten, how big a problem premature ejaculation was in their relationships. Here's a sample of their responses.

Torrie wrote:
I'm okay with premature ejaculation so for me it's a one... because nine times out of ten he can get hard again, within a short period of time. And it only takes me six minutes, so once that first waterfall rains I can do it repeatedly and fast.

Terri wrote:
The first encounter or when y'all haven't seen each other in a while and that tension has built up...not a problem at all. And remember y'all...we can't always control ourselves! But when he makes it last the next time...baaaaaby!

Gloria wrote:
For me it's a ten! Anticipation can cause it when you 1st get together from the anxiety of it all but...Houston we have a problem if this is business as usual. Women want to be pleased not teased it ain't all about pleasing the man. As a matter of fact, we should be climaxing together. That's it and that's all. 💯

Shante wrote:
He needs to be patient and address her needs first. There are techniques to help him prolong the act, but first there has to be honest communication about the problem. Too often, men won't acknowledge it as a regular occurrence, will dismiss it as an "oops" or worse, blame the woman. It is frustrating.

Cenia wrote:

Well, it is predicated on where we are in our relationship. First timer, he definitely gets a pass. If he is a long timer, my antennas will go up...if he has never shortchanged me before. I will be suspicious of him not being committed to our relationship. A female who is aware knows her man's sexual habits. When something appears to be out of the ordinary with his performance, we should be woman enough to try and discuss it with him. Because it just could be something that we are/are not doing to cause him to fail giving us a great ending.

Crystal wrote:

Ten, and I find that many men don't always respond with the maturity. And want to want to fix it...☹ it's disappointing for sure. Poor diets, won't speak to Dr. and act as if it's not their problem 👻.

Kwesha wrote:

Ladies we can't be so harsh on the first encounter. Remember there's an adjustment that has to be made between both parties. I mean let's keep a 💯. A lot of us don't bring our A game the 1st time either. Now okay be that critical if it keeps happening but its almost to be expected if he's a lil older (a meet & skeet) 😁

Melissa wrote:

It's only a big problem if they only got one in them... But if they can get it back up and finish me off, I'm good... Unfortunately, I've experienced that "one hitter quitter" *type dude a little too often and it's frustrating ASF! I always address it, but I get medical excuses, I'm tired, I'm done, yada yada yada... So now I just go ghost because I'm tired of the bullsh*t excuses. It's selfish ASF, especially when you don't try to rectify the problem.*

■ ■ ■

These responses were sincere and constructive. Now, you see why I always seek the female perspective to enhance my work. I learned a lot just from these comments. The first lesson is that most women understand men not performing optimally the first time or maybe the first few times. And two, women are most frustrated by men's unwillingness to fix the problem.

The title of this book, *Don't Lie To Me!*, was intentional. And the truth is some men lie about having dick control! As I see it, the solution to the problem is to start out slowly. I mean, what's the rush? You don't have to go hard out the gate. In fact, most women prefer that you ease into it. Better yet, start out with a long period of oral sex, and then she'll already be halfway there by the time you penetrate her. Remember, fellas, oral sex is your best friend!

Something else I learned on my journey to being a better lover is to avoid intense eye contact and kissing...if that's your trigger. I mean it! Sometimes gazing into a woman's eyes can cause you to explode. I know that was a trigger for me, especially when I was also kissing her on the lips! Also, laying directly on top of your partner can be a trigger, so instead, prop yourself up on your arms to minimize skin-to-skin contact. I know it seems trivial, but it works.

By the way, missionary is one of the worst for men who

want to control climaxing too soon because it's such an intimate position. My point is to try different positions to learn your triggers and then adapt accordingly.

Another exercise to prevent premature orgasms is to separate your mind from the physicality of the sex and instead focus on the mechanics. Allow me to explain the difference. Focusing on physicality is when you're sensitive to what you're feeling, such as the warmth of her vagina, the grip, and the sight of her body and beauty. Whereas "focusing on the technique" is when your attention is on using your body as a tool to please your partner. An example would be to think of a certain number of reps without counting aloud "1,2,3,4,5" but instead consciously adjusting your stroke to synchronize with her reaction, allowing her to lead you. Great sex is truly a dance!

Another critical factor in exercising self-control is controlling your breathing. If you allow yourself to get into a breathing pattern that escalates, it's a wrap! Men must learn to interrupt the rhythm of their breathing without throwing off the pace of the stroke. It takes practice, but you can learn to maintain the intensity of your stroke while changing your breathing pattern. Just take a deep breath, gather yourself, and exhale—*woo-sah*—and then get back to work!

Also, men can prolong sex by releasing a small amount of precum to knock the edge off while maintaining their stamina and erection. Again, it takes practice, but it's worth the effort if your goal is to please your woman and to rid yourself of sexual insecurity.

Oh, one last bit of advice for men with control issues, and I hope they'll put this at the top of their list; whatever you do, don't let that freak get on top! Once she's in the driver's seat, you're at her mercy!

Now let's address this issue about penis size once and for all!

■ ■ ■

STOP LYING BY SAYING "SIZE DOES MATTER!"

If we want to learn to be more transparent in our relationships, we must start being genuinely honest about the importance of men's penis size. That's not to say that a man needs a large penis, but it does need to be enough for that particular woman!

Why, then, do we beat around the bush instead of addressing this issue at the very beginning of the dating process? I mean, if the man doesn't have enough to please you, aren't you just wasting your time? And for those men who know they are challenged in that department, why torture yourself by falling for a woman who may need a long thick penis to be satisfied?

Look, I hate to sound so insensitive, but we're all grown here. What the hell are we waiting for before we have this talk? Now, if it truly doesn't matter how long, thick, or satisfying a man's penis is, then just skip to the next page, but if you're a woman who knows it takes a certain size to get you off, then it's your responsibility to speak up! Personally, I'd rather a woman just come right out and say, "Look, Michael, you're an interesting guy, and I'm very attracted to you, but large penises turn me on, and what you have is not enough!"

My response would be, "I appreciate your honesty, and although I love what I'm working with, I wish you the best in your search for your preference!"

See how simple that is? No harm done, and we get to remain friends. Sure, my ego would be a little bruised, but at least she will not be sexually frustrated for months, and my time and money won't be wasted. That's because she was upfront about her preference, and I was honest about the fact that I'm not packing—like that! Anytime a woman is explicit about needing a big one, she's not talking about six or seven inches but something long enough to pole-dance on, and I wish her the best in her search for Donkey Kong!

I'll never understand why adults who should know their sexual preferences and standards by forty aren't transparent and consistent about communicating it. As I've stated many times in this book, you can't get back the time you waste because of your lack of honesty. Not only do you waste your time but your partner's time.

I wondered if my followers would be bold enough to take on this issue. I was hesitant to post on my public Fan page because it was such an explicit topic, so I decided to post it in my private group, The Transparency Tribe. And just as I expected, my members confirmed how awkward a situation could become when you're not transparent about how important size really is! My post in the group read: Why do men lie about their dick size? And ladies, why not tell a man straight up that you require a certain size before you start dating? The point is men date with the intention of having sex, and I'm sure most women do too. So, if you know you require a big one, shouldn't that be communicated?

Here's what they had to say!

Sere wrote:
Here comes all the "size doesn't matter" folks ... yesterday's post where we were asked to share our worst sex stories was 90% of small dick stories ....so YES size does matter....stop lying to yourself that a shrimp size penis is fulfilling your sexual needs!

K Adore wrote:
I definitely think size matters and also knowing how to use it definitely matters. Sometimes you can have a man with a big dick, but he doesn't know how to wine in it and a guy that's smaller know how to wine in it. But if it's too small no matter how he wines you won't feel shit...unfortunately!

DrTanyka wrote:
Some men are in denial, even after you tell them...

Asley wrote:
Some of y'all guys be telling on yaself..talking about eating 🐱 from jump instead of throwing that 🍆 in my circle 👻 🌀 🌀 We know what that means.

Antione wrote:
I remember meeting this young lady on the dating site and she told me that her minimum was ten ins... And I remember thinking to myself "so man has to be at least a footlong for him to even fill a wall"... At least she was honest.

Melissa wrote:

As I got older (after 40) I began to wonder if it would be socially acceptable to ask a brotha to preview the equipment just to see if it meets the min criteria. Why waste each other's time or hurt someone's feelings or my own with disappointment and lack of fulfillment. I wish there was a way to do this that wouldn't make you an a**hole.

Ralph wrote:

Ain't no lying here...if she's one of those chicks that says some assassin shit like "I need 10 inches or more and make it hurt!" Mami is going to get this 8 inches and I can 👊 her in the face a few times to make it hurt and for each inch I'm short...to cover the spread. That's all she's got coming cuz that's all I got!

Valeria wrote:

I'm always honest about what I prefer and like sexually. The sad part is, men still lie about their dick size. One dude purchased Magnum even though he was about 4.5 inches 🤣 🤣 😊 He had to tie a knot in the mf. 😊 🤣 It was thick but not long enough and he knew that...I felt sorry for him.

Rosalind wrote:

I had what they call both ends of the stick! I was dating a man that was so big my hole couldn't conform to it. I admit, he warned me that he has put women in the hospital! Of course, I didn't believe him saying it was as big as my head! When it came time to get physically, whoa child! I thought he was wearing a strap on! I asked him to turn over! Before *that I tried pulling it! I swear it went past his kneecap! A magnum condom didn't fit! I couldn't do it! I didn't want to end up in the hospital!*

Then I had a dude that was a womanizer! How he got that title I don't know! He should have been a hermaphrodite! We went on a date, before I asked him to follow me to the gas station to get some gas. When we arrived at the gas station, he said he had to pee! He was a little tipsy, but this doesn't explain why he did what he did!

He took his penis out with two fingers! It looked like a baby penis; I was like omg! All these people looking at him and me! While he was pumping my gas, he was pissing all over his clothes with that thimble dick! I wanted to step on the gas! We were never intimate before and surely won't be intimate after that!

TaNisha wrote:
Met a man that told me straight up his penis was small and like a dummy I still choose to talk to him. I thought to myself, be cool get to know him, bc I'm thinking he's being over dramatic. I thought he was being modest. But the more I got to know him he would make jokes and reference to his penis being abnormally small it was starting to be excessive, really annoying like it was a real insecurity of his. So me being me, I asked for a picture 😒

Long story short (pun intended) he sent me a picture with a ruler, when I tell you he was hard, and it was a whopping

3 1/2 inches. I was honest and told him it was better for him to keep looking because I'm not her! Hunnnney I can and will not waste no more of yours or my time!

Sharifah wrote:
I tell 'em what I expect, and they better not lie cause I'm grabbing to make sure!

Anthony wrote:
That's one thing about me, I've never lied on my penis size. I would consider myself average size at best and I've never had any complaints. You don't need to be a porn star to satisfy a woman, that's for the movies!

I intentionally placed Sharifah's and Anthony's comments last. They were both transparent when it came to the size issue. Sharifah made her standards clear and was determined to ensure those standards were met. And Anthony let it be known that he's working with an average size, and women can either take it or leave it! I respect people who are transparent about what they want. You might get your feelings hurt and miss out on getting the person you want, but you're guaranteed not to waste your time!

Before we get into the topic of men having insecurities about sex toys, I want to address a couple of issues brought to my attention while writing this book. The first came about when one of my male followers deflected on the size issues by accusing some women of having vaginas that were "stretched out" because they had too many sex partners! Some men were bold enough to ask women in the group about their body count as if a high number would determine a woman's ability to be satisfied with an average size penis.

Now, I understand why an insecure man would wonder about a woman's number, but I can't come up with one good reason why he would actually come out and ask it. Yes, some men think about a woman's body count, particularly if they're serious about the relationship, but not to the extent of drilling her about it, and certainly not to the point of making it a determining factor on whether or not to pursue her. Either you're sexually satisfied with a woman, or you're not! There's no sense in belittling her just because of your insecurities or because your dick is too small.

Some men are triggered to ask this question because the woman may have what he considers to be a large vagina. Or maybe she gets really wet during intercourse, or there's not enough friction, or it could be a combination of both. Well, my suggestion is for the man to either offer to pay for vaginal rejuvenation, leave her alone, or keep his insecurities to himself! What he should not do, and what the woman should not allow him to do, is demean her by suggesting that she's "used up!"

This is the classic double standard that drives women crazy! While men want to sew their oats all over town, hell, all over the world, they expect women to be celibate or at least restrict their vaginas to an acceptable number of penises. Acceptable to him, to be exact, which is bullshit! And if we're keeping it real, it doesn't matter to some men if the woman is tight as a vice grip. He's still going to trip over how many men she's been with. But why? All he should be concerned about is that he's getting it now!

But if you're a man lying about being sexually secure when you're not, then all your sexual inadequacies get projected onto your partner. Not only is she made to feel defensive and ashamed of whatever her number is, but the man often resorts to verbal abuse because she doesn't know how to deal with feeling "less than."

This problem of body-count shaming is exaggerated by men with erectile dysfunction. I understand how ED can play on a man's psyche and ego. For a short period, I had some performance issues due to my diabetes. It didn't impact my ability to get or maintain an erection, but it made having sex uncomfortable. Now, this only lasted a few weeks because I made an appointment with my doctor as soon as possible. But for those twenty or so days, I'm not going to lie, it really fucked with me. Not being able to perform to the level you're accustomed to as a man is emasculating. The woman, unaware of the problem, just assumes you're tired or, worse, that you're no longer attracted to her.

But here's where I don't understand some men: the moment I had an inkling that something was off, I went into panic mode! So, if men feel emasculated, as I did, why not do something about it immediately instead of asking a woman about how many penises she's had inside of her vagina or accusing her of cheating, which is usually what follows? Again, instead of addressing the root of the problem, some men with ED try to flip their trauma onto their partners!

I've discussed this topic many times on my social media pages and in detail in the last chapter, so I'm not going to go into it again except for one comment made by one of my followers named Shaun. Her comment speaks to the pain that so many women experience when men are in denial about their ED instead of confronting the problem.

Shaun wrote:

I wasn't given a chance to handle it! When I tried to talk to him about it and comfort him, he faked sleep. Then the next day he picked a fight. After that we went our separate ways. Sometime later (months later) I told him I still cared for him and if there was something troubling him, he could talk to me. He opened up a little hinting around but never confessed to it. So, even after all that we have been through, he just couldn't be honest! Women are more understanding when you tell them the truth! Besides, we already suspect, or even know, that you have a problem so hiding only hurts more.

■ ■ ■

I want men to know that women who think like Shaun are the rule, not the exception. The idea that women need men who are sex machines and will "sex them down" 24-7 is a myth. Most mature women want love, commitment, affection, consistency, and transparency. And they also want to help.

No woman in her right mind will throw away a good man just because he has ED issues, but he must stop lying about it being an issue. Unless he can do that, I advise women to find someone else because it will only be a matter of time before he deflects from his own laziness and starts accusing you of stepping out, which some women ultimately do after years of being denied sex because of her man's stubbornness against seeking help. I'm not saying it's right. In fact, cheating is always wrong, but dammit, I understand!

Okay, it's time to talk about sex toys! Yeah!

■ ■ ■

THAT DAMN ROSE!
Sex Toys & Sexual Insecurity

They're called sex "toys" for a reason! They're supposed to be fun and exciting, not traumatizing. Now, I can understand how a man would feel "some kind of way" if his woman whipped out a thick 10-inch black dildo and started going to work the first time they had sex. That's not a red flag. That's a flashing red siren! Women should give their partners a chance to get acquainted with their vaginas before they break out the dildos, rabbits, roses, sledgehammers, or whatever the hell they call these new gadgets!

Sometimes, it's not what you do but how you do it. I believe sex toys should be introduced into the bedroom once the couple develops a rapport. How else can you know the best way to enhance your sex life if you don't know what you're working with? No man wants to have his woman frantically reaching for her rose the first few times they have sex. The message to him is, "Get out the way, loser. I'll handle this myself!" I'm sure women wouldn't appreciate their man reaching for an artificial vagina on the nightstand and then jerking off during their first night of sex. How you introduce a sex toy can determine how your partner receives it.

Now, I'm not implying that women should wait months to include her rose and other toys into the sexual equation, but it would be wise to take some time to learn your partner's level of security. Some guys are okay coming out the gate with sex toys, squirting, choking, yellow showers, etc. But let's be honest; most men will not be cool with that. So, if you're a woman who likes to get the party cracking with games and toys from day one, then let that be known. Don't just spring the freak on a man by handcuffing him to the headboard and then slap him on the ass with a whip, yelling, "It's Play-time!"

Seriously, though, I think it would be helpful if a woman explained to her partner before having sex that toys are meant to enhance their experience, not to compensate for him coming up short. Ladies, demonstrate to him how much pressure you like and what motions to use. And teach him how to bring you to climax. Men like to feel accomplished in bed, whether he's doing all the work or being directed.

Now, I know some of you ladies will say, "Michael, these men are too insecure to learn!" And I agree that some of us can be close-minded and naive. We've been taught from watching pornography that the moment we insert our penis into a woman, she is transported to the fifth dimension of ecstasy. Not understand that a woman can bring herself to more intense pleasure and frequent orgasms simply because she knows how to hit her spots. It often has nothing to do with what the man is doing or not doing.

It took me some time in my own relationships to under-stand that. One partner, in particular, rarely reached orgasm from the anal, vaginal, or oral stimulation. Some women are just made that way. But give her a toy, and she could work magic! I'm sure had we stayed together longer, her orgasms would have become more frequent, but my attitude was, "It is what it is!" Now, do I think I could've been happy with that situation longer term? No, I don't. I prefer a woman who can climax regularly with or without toys. Call it the male ego!

Having said that, some men will never be okay with their woman using sex toys. In their minds, the rose is the enemy, not a friend. Any orgasm that he does not produce is cheating. "Why do you need sex toys anyway when you have me?" he'll say. Or, "Using vibrators will desensitize your clitoris and make it impossible for you to climax once you get a man!" These are the lies inexperienced or insecure men tell themselves to justify blocking you. So, ladies, you've got a choice to make with these kinds of men. It's either going to be him or your toys—you can't have both!

Some women are reading this and saying, "Shit, you must be crazy! You may as well get to steppin' cause these toys and I have been through some hard times together!" (pun intended). And to those ladies, I say, "Do you! No one should have to give up their pleasures because of someone else's old-fashioned thinking and insecurities."

Women are sick and tired of catering to men's inability to keep up. For an increasing number of them, it's not enough to be sexually compatible. They want a sexually adventurous man! Many of them are at the point where they refuse to hide their kinks or their toys. Hell, some of y'all have sex rooms and dungeons at home.

This reminds me of when I was writing this chapter. My sister happened to send me a link to share with my followers about a show on Netflix called *How To Build A Sex Room*. It's hosted by a sixty-year-old woman who comes into couple's homes and sets them up with sex rooms. For the record, my sister is a Scorpio, so I wasn't too surprised, but I haven't looked at her or my mild-mannered brother-in-law the same ever since.

I'm glad my brother-in-law and my other male associates are open to their partners exploring their sexuality with role-playing, toys, sex swings, and all kinds of fun gadgets. And it's great to be able to post about it in my groups and have both men and women respond with an open mind. I always emphasize how important it is to live your life to the fullest, and being able to express your true sexual self is a vital part of that! Here are some comments from my group on the insecurities some people have about sex toys. I also inquired whether women would consider cheating or leaving their partners if they didn't have sex toys as a backup!

Michael wrote:
I've never met a woman that "requires" a toy to climax but me and my woman do use them. I never had a problem with it because I realize that there are different types of orgasms. The one's i give her are going to be from deep penetration, rubbing her G spot with my fingers, or giving some slow and superb tongue action. Her vibrator is going to give her a totally different feel and orgasm and it's awesome to see.

Sometimes me, her, and her dildo will have threesome and I'll use it to penetrate her while I recharge or before I even get started. Moral of the story is toys are your friend and only an insecure man would have a problem with them.

Antione wrote:
As a man I wouldn't look my woman needs toys the climax. I will look at it more like what toys can I use on her to help her climax even harder. You can fulfill a lot of fantasies

with some massage oils, good music, a candle, a blindfold and several toys.

Linda Ashford wrote:

I would ask why isn't she able to climax with her partner? If that is what she needs in order to climax, then he should use them on her and assist. Typically, this is just a clitoral climax one of the easiest to achieve if you ask me...
Another question that I would ask is: "Can she make herself orgasm?" We can not expect others to do for us what we can not do for ourselves.

Onetyme wrote:

Hmmmm.....it can affect her ability to have an orgasm with the real deal if over used. However, I think toys offer diversity and can add to the sexual adventure of all involved. No cheating needed.

Sere wrote:

I went six years without dating and 🍭. I used my toys 3-4 times per week during the six years I didn't get no D! Several months ago I started a "fun" summer fling and I've had no problems having orgasms or multiple orgasms every time my summer lover visits me.

So, for me that's a big fat NO! Using them nonstop for years has not affected my ability to orgasm...people need to stop blaming the toys for their whack ass sex sessions!

Joelyn wrote:
The real question is not about the toy. The real question is if she is connecting and pleased buy the sexual connection between, she and her partner. Sometimes in relationship if someone is truly unhappy or if their partner is not pleasing them due to a lack of experience or lack of stamina there is a possibility of cheating.

The toy is an attempt in those situations to receive full pleasure. With a partner who completely satisfies you, toys can enhance your pleasure. Most of the time people don't cheat because the sex is horrible, you can tell by the comments and hear that most people will rather leave the person alone if the sex is whack!

There's usually something missing in the intimacy or in the relationship part. And the truth is there are men that are intimidated by toys especially if she's more attracted to the toy than him.

Key wrote:
I am not a toy fan, they frustrate me. I just don't have the skill or the imagination to use them properly! Most women would take the real thing over a toy any day! The only "advantage" to a toy is being able to get what she needs to get her there, placement, pressure and longevity. Men would do the same thing if asked. Well, mine does. No need to cheat!

Delvin wrote:
When my wife sold Bedroom Kandi, women would often say "I'd love to buy some toys, but my husband/boyfriend would freak out." Dudes really not about that life, quite sad really.

Carla wrote:
Tell him it's either the Toys or it's gonna be the Boys! Which would you rather me entertain? lol

Defontae wrote:
I'm not killing myself. I'm going to bring the toy for her.

■ ■ ■

It's easy to be insecure about using sex toys at the beginning of a relationship, but if you have a woman who goes hard in the paint—all the time, which most do—you'll be happy to have the rose as a backup. That's the kind of threesome I'm down for every time.

Before we move on, I think it's important to mention that men who exhibit these kinds of insecurities tend to have a lot of underlining issues. Some I've mentioned include having ED, issues with not controlling their orgasms, and size issues. But many of them are also suffering from emotional scars from abandonment, verbal and sexual abuse, and trauma from being cheated on. Any challenge to their manhood is a trigger to past pain. To those men, and the women who are involved with them, stop lying to yourselves by ignoring it. The worst thing you can do when you witness sexual insecurity is to allow it to fester.

Insecurity breaks you down to the worst version of yourself and keeps you in a place of constant criticism and avoidance. And by avoidance, I mean not facing the truth that you are insecure. That's when the anxiety sets in. And because of your unwillingness to stop lying to yourself, you lash out, sometimes violently. It's terrible to watch an otherwise kind person be diminished and defeated by their insecurities.

As someone who has been a part of the media for over twenty-five years, I know its influence on what men view as being a man. But those images of masculinity are created to sell you something—they are not real. Neither is it real that all women want rich, tall, dark men with 10-inch penises who could make them orgasm 24-7. If that were true, there would be a whole lot of single women out there. The truth is most women are in relationships with, and love, men who are nowhere near rich and whose penises are an average of 5.1 to 5.5 inches. Yes, that average size male penis.

So, relax, fellas, stop watching so much pornography, and start having real conversations with women about what they really want. Yes, some women desire deep penetration, oral sex, sex toys, multiple orgasms, sex two or three times a day, and being kinky at times. Still, they mostly want a man who is consistent, transparent, funny, passionate, romantic, and someone they can learn from and can introduce them to new experiences. A man who reads, follows politics, and travels the world will always be more interesting to mature women than a man whose only asset is packing a big penis!

Instead of defining manhood by obsessing over tapping "that ass," men might want to focus on stamping that passport!

STOP LYING ABOUT BEING MONOGAMOUS

The alternative to lying about loving and having sex with multiple partners is being honest about it. That's the only aspect of alternative relationships I'm interested in promoting.

Most people don't possess the time, energy, or communication to maintain one healthy relationship, let alone two, three, or more.

But if you're truly interested in moving away from a life of lies to become transparent, that journey begins with one profound step; admitting to yourself that you're not monogamous and moving accordingly.

14

WHAT IS ETHICAL NON-MONOGAMY?

I want you to ask your male and female friends a question. Ask them if they consider a man "a better man" simply because he's monogamous. What about a woman who only loves or has sex with one man at a time? Is she automatically considered to be a "better" woman?

Wouldn't it be fairer to say that a person is more compatible with someone seeking a monogamous relationship but not necessarily better? The point I'm making is that monogamy is only one characteristic out of many that make someone compatible with you. It may be a major factor, maybe even a deal breaker, but it's not the only thing to consider when choosing a partner.

Here's a list of traits that I think are just as important as monogamy:

Physical attraction, chemistry, honesty, consistency, hygiene, temperament, relationship with parents and children, how they manage money, debt, work ethic, compatible lifestyles, lifestyle, religious beliefs, history of abuse, sexual health, and general health, just to name a few.

But the most important characteristic that should be top of your list when choosing a partner is acceptance. In other words, the ability to be your true self with your partner. The truth is most people, especially men, choose monogamy to appease their partner. And the same is true for some women who are non-monogamous but understand that most men will never accept their truth.

And that's the beauty of having a partner who is ethically non-monogamous. The promise of monogamy is a nonfactor, which, in turn, makes the other qualities I mentioned even more important. Society has programmed us to prioritize monogamy to such a degree that qualities such as temperament, mental health, and the ability to handle adversity are not even considered. As long as they promise to only have sex with you, "It's all good!" But is it? Remember, I said "a promise of monogamy," not necessarily the reality of monogamy. We'll get to that later.

Another benefit of ethical non-monogamy is not having the expectation of getting rid of people that enhance your life! Whomever you love, is a true friend, or simply makes you happy is not asked to leave. Anything or anyone that adds to your life should remain in your life, whether you are sexually involved with them or not.

How many of us have made the mistake of discarding people we cared about, who loved us, or who brought us comfort just because someone new came along and demanded? Or maybe we decide to dump them because we've been taught that it's the proper thing to do! Whatever the reason, most often, we end up regretting it. Most romantic relationships don't last. So, we run back to the person who's already proven their loyalty, apologize for cutting them off, and try to rekindle the relationship. Sometimes we succeed, but those ties are often broken forever because they no longer trust that we won't do it again.

This tradition of throwing away valuable people just because someone new comes into the scene is reckless, immature, and unwise. The new person hasn't proven anything except that they are attracted to you, whereas the person who has been in your life has demonstrated love, consistency, and loyalty. But the minute someone with a pretty face comes along promising to love only you and fuck only you, we've been taught the proper thing to do is throw everyone else aside. And that's cool if they have no value. But remember this, when you meet someone, or when they meet you, the person they are attracted to is who they are and where they are in large part because of their other partners. Whether it's a relationship that provides incredible sex or emotional and financial support, the person you meet is the sum of everyone contributing to their life. So, explain to me with reason; why are they being dismissed?

I want to emphasize—with reason! Not emotions, and not what someone else expects or societal standards, but what makes sense? I think it demonstrates intelligence to keep every resource possible that adds to your life! Don't cut people off for no reason except the ego and insecurity of a new partner, especially when the person already in your life is absolutely fine with you adding someone new without conditions and ultimatums. That's a true friend to me—that's real love!

People claim to love you, but the whole idea of a conventional monogamous relationship is to possess you. "You're mine!" you hear lovers say. "You belong to me!" That sounds cute until insecurity sets in, and you begin to regret the idea of being someone's property. Ethical non-monogamy says you're your own person, and your love is yours to share freely, not yours to own. But instead of accepting your partner for who they are and who they love, people in conventional relationships seek to fix, alter, and influence their partners to do what they want them to do. They want to create a version of you they are comfortable with. Your happiness is secondary to their insecurity being made more secure.

Let's keep it real. People don't come into conventional relationships seeking to give but rather for what they can get! They don't accept you—they want to improve you. Their objective isn't for you to be happy as a couple but to make themselves happy and, in the process, change the version of you they were attracted to in the first place! It's crazy, right?

They want to change how you dress, eat, and wear your hair and dictate who your friends are. And if you're living together, some of them expect you to go to bed at the same time they do. What in The Mr. Potato Head is going on here?!

Love is freedom! Freedom to be yourself, freedom to come and go as you please, freedom to love who you want, freedom to choose who to invest your time in. And just because someone chooses to live their life with others shouldn't diminish you; only you can! Being valued has nothing to do with someone being exclusive to you! If that were true, every woman in a monogamous relationship would feel special and whole, and we know they don't. The truth is, just as many women in relationships feel alone as those living single. Maybe even more so!

WHAT IS ETHICAL NON-MONOGAMY?

I love ethical non-monogamy because it sets you and your partner free! And that should be the objective of entering into a relationship. What do I mean by setting free? I mean, both of you are free to come and go as you please, free to have friends of the opposite sex, free to call or not call, and free to do everything you were doing when you met.

When I meet a woman, I don't feel I have the authority to decide who stays in her life, whether she's having sex with them or if they're close friends. That's her choice because it's her body and her life. Besides, how can you ever get to know someone if you don't allow them to do whatever they want to do? Then you can judge if that's the kind of person you want to be with. Show me the real you, and let me decide if I want to fuck with you! It's that simple!

Ethical non-monogamy means being honest about who you're emotionally and sexually involved with or if you see the potential for a situation to go deeper. All parties involved are made aware of others you are involved with and the depth of those situations. If they decide to stay, based on your truth, they consent to you continuing to see other people—that's it!

If you really think about it, most of us have practiced ethical non-monogamy during dating. We assume the person we're interested in is talking to or having sex with others, or they tell us outright, and we continue to see them; that's consent!

ENM is an umbrella term for being involved romantically or intimately in two or more relationships that are non-exclusive! But here's the part most people always seem to leave out—it's consensual. That means no surprises, no tricks, and no omissions. Everyone involved is informed and signs off.

ENM is the opposite of monogamy, where two partners are exclusive to one another both sexually and emotionally. There's no one else! A monogamous relationship is what we're raised to accept as the norm. Most of our parents saw it as the best and only way to conduct a relationship. Your mission in life was to go to school, get a job, find "The One," and live happily ever after—'til death do us part! But were we sold a fantasy? I'll address that later.

It's important to point out that there is another form of non-monogamy that isn't ethical. Some people become intimately involved with another partner without consent and don't inform any of the parties involved. In other words, unethical non-monogamy is cheating. However, ethically non-monogamy isn't cheating because, again, there must be consent by everyone involved when someone new comes into the picture, emotionally or sexually. For whatever reason, some people can't wrap their minds around this basic concept of being transparent.

As I stated earlier, most of us have been raised to see our

partners as our possessions. And we've also been conditioned to lie about our feeling for those who are not our partners. The idea that someone could be open and honest about loving more than one person without hiding it is hard for most people to grasp. Or maybe they don't want to grasp it because it doesn't benefit them to be open to it. When you mention ENM to a woman, the most common response is, "If you love someone else, you need to go and be with her!" I'll respond to that shortly. Let's continue.

Changing how people define a relationship requires more than an open mind; it requires a whole paradigm shift. But most people are too afraid or unwilling to consider taking a different path, even when their current way of thinking has failed them for most of their lives. And you know what they say about people who do the same thing repeatedly, expecting a different result? But I want to "go there," at least not yet!

A paradigm shift is defined as *"an important change that happens when the usual way of thinking about or doing something is replaced by a new and different way."*

I think people have no problem changing how they think as long as that change benefits them. But once they understand that thinking differently sets their partner free, suddenly, change is too hard!

Society has programmed us into believing there's only one way to love, one kind of love, and only one objective—finding that special someone and settling down! But what if you choose to love differently? And what if your definition of settled down involves doing it with more than one person? Who's right and who's wrong? And most importantly, who gets to decide that for you and me?

Isn't it interesting that from birth, we've been taught that monogamy is the best way, hell, the only way to be happy and fulfilled? But even with all the examples of marriage and observing couples in our families, in the media, as well as religious teachings, we can't manage to get half of the people who get married to stay married. And that goes for the Bible thumpers as well as atheists!

If we measured the success of institutional marriage by the same standard as we do to grade elementary school homework, it would be considered a failure. We should not be satisfied or remain silent while society flaunts a fifty percent divorce rate as something to aspire to. And don't even get me started about how many couples out of that 50% stay together because of financial obligations or for the sake of the kids. But that's a whole other book!

Look, I'm not suggesting ethical non-monogamy is for everyone, but monogamy obviously isn't working out so well for everyone either! And what's so frustrating is that you can't even bring up the subject of ethical non-monogamy around the average person without them getting defensive. I jokingly say to them, "Nobody's trying to recruit you, but can we at least talk about it?"

But monogamy has been engrained into society to the point where people can't even entertain having a conversation about it. Sadly, people are stuck no matter how disastrous the outcome is. It's hard to give up on the fantasy of the church wedding, tropical honeymoon, the 2.5 kids, a boy and a girl, and the house with the white picket fence. Most people still hold on to that traditional vision. Hell, I sometimes question whether I still want a "normal" monogamous lifestyle. As I said, the programming is hard to shake.

But maybe it's not about "shaking" the idea of monogamy. Maybe it's about transitioning into and out of whatever relationship dynamic suits you during that particular chapter of your life. The more options of love styles you have to choose from, the better your chances of finding someone you click with! As the saying goes, timing is everything!

So, I know you're wondering why anyone would choose to be ethically non-monogamous. I'm not talking about the non-monogamy that happens when you first meet. As I said, most couples are non-monogamous at the beginning of the dating process. But why would anyone choose ethical non-monogamy once they become emotionally and sexually involved?

Well, if you keep an open mind, you might learn something applicable whether you choose ENM or not. What's fundamental to this lifestyle is complete transparency. And I think we would all agree that whatever relationship dynamic you're pursuing, honesty is in short supply.

WHY WOULD ANYONE CHOOSE ETHICAL NON-MONOGAMY?

Well, if you keep an open mind, you might learn something applicable whether you choose ENM or not. What's fundamental to this lifestyle is complete transparency. And I think we would all agree that whatever relationship dynamic you're pursuing, honesty is in short supply.

People who engage in ethical non-monogamy may have a partner who doesn't meet their other needs. They love their primary partner, but something may be missing, something they simply don't want to live without.

But whatever "that thing" is that's missing, that person has decided it isn't worth throwing away everything else that's working in their relationship. And that's precisely what we've been taught to do! Dump the person who can't satisfy our every need and find someone who will. Good luck with that!

Earlier, I told you about the typical responses I get from monogamous women when I present them with the question, "How would you respond if your partner admitted they wanted also to spend time with someone else, but you knew without a doubt they loved or valued you?"

Most women would reply, "If you love someone else, you should leave me and go be with them!"

But why should I have to leave you? ENM has nothing to do with your partner not being happy. They just want more, I try to explain to them, not just more sex but more of whatever that other person provides that you may not.

I hate using this example of polyamory, but it's relative and valid. We're all polyamorous when it comes to loving more than one friend, more than one parent, more than one child, and even more than one pet. Why is that understandable until the issue of loving more than one intimate partner is included in that example? Why do otherwise reasonable people shut down and get defensive when a practical point has been made? Whether this lifestyle is for you or not, can't we agree that practicing polyamory happens every day? All I'm asking is for people to put their defenses down, and let's be sensible and hash this out!

I'm willing to have a conversation about the relevance of the examples I argued for if they're willing to talk about the similarities. Then we can come to a concession about what works and doesn't work for that individual.

But again, the programming is deep. This is what I wrote earlier about how we're raised to believe. I said, "Our mission in life is to find "The One" and settle down forever—'til death do us part!

Is finding "The One" that God made for you a worthwhile goal or a fantasy? Don't you think most people who get married think they've found "The One?" Or maybe the second wife is "The One?" Or the third husband? Come on, people. "The One" may be the "The One" right now, for where you are at that stage in your life. Can a person truly be "The One" if it doesn't last? Or are there several "Ones" in your life? If the latter is true, then there is no such thing as "The One!"

Before I go on, I want to clarify that I believe in marriage. In fact, all my close friends are happily married. Some have cheated in the past, and some are married to women who used to be their side chicks. And some make me give them the side eye, wondering if they're swinging on the down low. Now, I couldn't tell you if all of them are currently practicing ethical non-monogamy, but I know they all have solid relationships. So, I'm not anti-marriage or anti-monogamy. I want to make sure I'm clear on that.

But I also want to be clear that even monogamous marriages can include a little "playtime!" In other words, that couple may want to spice things up occasionally by inviting someone into their bedroom. And I bet most monogamous people would judge them for just having fun, even though their relationship is monogamous 99% of the time. And that's another reason people choose ENM. There's no expectation that your partner must fulfill every need that you have for the relationship to work...forever!

Expecting your partner to do it all and be it all is why those who are into ENM feel less pressure and more security; their partners don't have to end the relationship for them to experience something different, or as some refer to it, "Getting something strange!"

Expecting your partner to be the best at oral sex, vaginal sex, and anal sex and the best kisser, conversationalist, hang-out buddy, muse, supporter, and someone who loves you in a way that you never want to love anyone else is, I think, a recipe for disaster. Those kinds of unrealistic expectations ultimately lead to pain, disappointment, and a complete breakdown of the relationship.

But when you allow people to be their authentic selves, to be ethical about loving and desiring others, it offers them the chance to explore things you may not be interested in. That's not to say that your relationship is not working. It's merely an opportunity to gain more happiness and fulfillment from others to strengthen your relationship. The harsh truth is that many relationships wouldn't stand a chance of lasting without side pieces. That's right, I said it!

I truly believe that ethical non-monogamy can strengthen a relationship by allowing you and your partner to express yourself in ways you could not ordinarily do in a conventional monogamous relationship. Having that freedom to express yourself and to have your partner supporting you is a more genuine expression of love than someone who believes true love means only loving their partner.

We must stop lying to ourselves about being monogamous or about our partners being monogamous and really start talking about what we want without worrying about being judged or the threat of losing someone we value.

But here's where the hard work really needs to be done. We must acknowledge that some people have more love to give, which has nothing to do with what we're not giving them. When parents decide to have more than one child, no one questions it. Why? Yes, it should be based on what they can afford, but it's mainly because they decided they had more love to give.

We embrace new friends because we have more or different interests that we don't share even with our best friend. And many of us also have strong emotional and sexual feelings toward more than one person simultaneously. Why should we lie to ourselves and our partners and suppress that?

The point of this book is to challenge people to be more transparent and let the chips fall. You might be surprised that your partner may be more open than you think. Relationships are more likely to survive and thrive with ENM because you don't have to end one relationship to start another. It's not greed, it's natural, and it's with consent! And let me emphasize that many relationships are non-sexual.

But be warned, ENM is not for those who have broken and distrustful relationships—it doesn't fix anything! I only recommend this journey for solid couples looking to grow together, not grow apart. It requires maturity, great communication skills, and complete transparency. The bottom line is if you can't manage a monogamous relationship, you won't be successful at ethical non-monogamy either. So, don't even bother.

Other considerations are your availability to date and manage more than one partner. Ask yourself, "Do I have the time?

Do I have the financial resources? Do I possess good conflict resolution skills?" because you're going to need them. And most critically, "Do I have trust issues?" People think these relationships are all about sex, but just as with monogamous relationships, sex is rarely the foundation that keeps people together. I'll be touching on the sexual myths surrounding polyamory in the next chapter.

THE WORLD OF ETHICAL NON-MONOGAMY

Polyamory is just one of many love styles under the umbrella of ethical non-monogamy. If you'd like to be educated about the different labels and terminology of the ENM lifestyle, continue with the rest of this chapter. For those who are ready to dive into the next chapter on polyamory, just move forward a few pages. But I think you'll find the labels interesting. I've been poly for years, and I hadn't heard half of these terms. Enjoy and Learn!

Ethical Non-monogamy (ENM) – an umbrella term that encompasses polyamory, open relationships, solo poly, relationship anarchy

Polyamory – (Poly = many, Amory = love) – Practice of engaging in multiple relationships simultaneously with consent and knowledge of all parties (may or may not include sexual activity)

Polygamist/Polygamy/Polygny – 1 man with multiple women. These women do not have other men, and they do not have sex with one another

Polygamist/Polygamy/Polyandry – 1 woman with multiple men, and they do not have sex with one another

Triad/Trouple – 3 partners romantically and or sexually involved with one another

Closed Triad – 3 people involved with one another, and their gender doesn't matter

Open Triad – 3 people having a relationship together and also dating others as well

Solo Poly – Open to dating/engaging in multiple meaningful relationships without having a primary partner, one person to whom they're committed above all other partners

OPP – One Penis Policy / One Pussy Policy

KTP – Kitchen Table Poly – Having multiple partners and your preference is for them to know one another and hang out and possibly live together at some point

Parallel Poly – You are aware of other partners but prefer not to interact with them

DADT Polyamory – "Don't ask, Don't tell"

Nesting Partner – 1 or more partners you choose to live with

V or Hinge Poly – 1 person in a relationship with 2 people who know each other but are not in a relationship with others

Unicorn – A person who dates couples only

Unicorn Hunters – Couples who seek a partner who must date/have sex with both of them

Hierarchical relationships – When an existing relationship takes precedence over another

Veto Power – Mainly used by couples who see each other as their primary partners. One/both partners have the option to forbid or block the other from dating or continuing their relationship with a specific person

Metamour – Your partner's other partner with whom you are not dating

Sister wives – The women in the relationship whose relationship is platonic

Relationship anarchist – No labels. Each relationship has different ideals that work for them, i.e., shared income or one may have a child together, etc

Threesome – Any 3 people engaging sexually

Bi-sexual – They have sex with both genders

Bi-romantic – They have sex and are romantic with both genders

Monogamish – You and your partner have agreed that while you don't identify as poly, you aren't 100% close to other partners either

Compersion – The opposite of jealousy. Experiencing joy/happiness when your partner is happy about their partner (metamour)

Ambiamorous – A person who is comfortable being in a mono/poly relationship

Anchor Partner – A partner you are practically or logically involved with, living with, married to, or have children with, or someone who emotionally grounds you and is someone you rely on for a long-term partnership!

■ ■ ■

I know what you're thinking: "Wow!" That was my reaction too. There's so much to learn whether you're in the lifestyle or not. And there are so many preconceived notions. I can't wait to get into some of them next!

When you tell people that you're poly, they become apprehensive. Most have no idea what it means, but that doesn't stop them from being judgmental.

Others are intrigued and immediately begin asking questions, while others cut the conversation short and run for the hills! And then you have those who pretend to be okay with your poly life just to get next to you, but that never lasts.

So, if you think it's hard for you "normal" folks to find a compatible partner, just imagine what non-monogamous people are going through. It's tough out here in these poly streets!

15

POLY LIFE

Let me be clear; I am not a poly guru! However, I pride myself on being a resource for those who want to move away from a life of lies and drama and evolve into being more transparent. And like many of you, I'm curious about how others navigate their poly relationships! Sure, I've had my own experiences over the past thirty years, but what you'll quickly learn about polyamory is that everyone's experience is different, and there are many types of polyamory love styles.

Polyamory is simply being honest, transparent, responsible, and non-possessive in the way you approach your relationships. It means loving multiple people simultaneously and being clear about your intentions. And here's the critical part—it's all done with consent.

Being polyamorous is a conscious choice to have many partners. Sometimes those partners may engage with each other socially or not know anything about one another except that they exist. Also, being polyamorous means having romantic relationships that may or may not involve sex with more than one person at a time. And the sexual orientation of those other partners may vary.

But unlike open relationships, polyamory is not just sexual; the partners are emotionally involved. Again, everyone is informed about who is in the picture and how deep their emotions go, even if they don't meet or know the details about who the other partners are.

A common question people ask about poly life is, "Who comes first when you have multiple partners?" Well, that depends. Some polyamorous relationships are hierarchical, meaning one relationship takes priority over the others. And other times, they are equal, which basically means you get in where you fit in!

Most people tend to only focus on the sexual aspects of polyamorous relationships because, for them, that's the only way they can process the idea of a relationship that's not just between one man and one woman. But I also think people focus on sex because it's the easiest aspect of polyamory to attack. They completely bypass any possible benefits and focus on how much sex they'll be losing out on as if they're having all this great sex in the first place. Their obsession with sex between multiple partners is often a defense mechanism that speaks to either their insecurity due to the lack of sexual satisfaction in their monogamous relationships or their possessive nature, which we'll discuss later.

But polyamorous relationships are so much more dynamic than just sex. Remember, these are not open relationships or swingers where emotionally detached sex is the objective. Although you can be a swinger and be polyamorous, most poly relationships are about cultivating emotional connections. It takes much more than physical attraction and multiple orgasms to maintain these partnerships.

Taking on the responsibility of loving two or more people is no small task. The sexual demands are challenging, no doubt, especially when dealing with multiple partners with healthy sex drives. The first few months of having freaky three-somes are awesome, but over time, that can drain even the most virile person who is expected to please both partners. I'm not saying the passion dies, but the frequency and intensity may decrease.

Then there are the emotional and conversational needs of each partner. Depending on whether everyone lives together or apart, you'll find yourself having to repeat the same conversations if there's no interaction between the partners. To avoid being redundant, ideally, the partners should at least engage in phone calls regularly to be kept in the loop about what's going on in each other's lives. While parallel poly dynamics are more of the norm in my experience, poly relationships work best when there is some engagement with the partners. But again, that's my experience.

And finally, there's the financial responsibility of dating more than one woman or a woman who's involved and providing for two or more men if she's the breadwinner. Relationships cost! I don't care how frugal you are. When once-a-week dinner dates turn into twice a week or more, you'll feel it in your pocket. Not every woman is going to be satisfied with Applebee's and Red Lobster. Suppose you set the standard of taking her to Ruth Chris and The Capitol Grille. In that case, it's a reasonable expectation that that level of dining will continue or whatever you're offering financially.

Now, I know some people will assume that just because you're poly doesn't mean you should be expected to provide equally for each partner, and I agree with that—to a degree! But if you present yourself as a poly man to Woman One, for example, and you've been wining and dining her for, let's say, six months, and then you meet Woman Two, shouldn't Woman One assume nothing will change with regards to your level of dating? I think that's reasonable.

You see, it's all fun and games when you're sneaking around without any accountability, but when you're in a real relationship with multiple people, it requires time management, financial resources, effort, patience, and understanding each person's needs and listening to their problems, their triggers, and consistency. In short, you gotta have skills!

So, if you can't manage one relationship, what makes you think you can handle two or more? Most people are delusional about being able to manage a poly life. It's interesting hearing some men talking about the poly life as if it's only about being honest about having sex with multiple women. But it's about much more—don't sleep! Being in a full-blown relationship with two mature women is not for the weak! And neither is dealing with two or more grown men. Many women can hang sexually with multiple male partners, but do they want the emotional responsibility? Men can be needy, possessive, and a pain in the ass. But let's start with the topic of men who think they want to be poly.

Women have needs. And multiple partners have multiple needs. A man's ability to step up and provide resources is critical in any type of relationship but especially in the poly world, whether that's in the form of finances, commitment, communication, maturity, inspiration, emotional support, consistency, and the ability to satisfy multiple women, especially those over forty, sexually! No easy task, let me tell you!

Before men step into real poly life, they need to understand that today's woman is not accepting weak, inconsistent sex, especially when she has agreed to share her man. Women today are exercising, eating healthily, going to spin classes, hiking, jogging, and doing hot yoga, whatever the hell that is! And statistically, women over forty are in their sexual prime—they can go all night! I can guarantee you that most men haven't thought this whole poly thing through sexually. Most men are delusional about their ability to manage two whole relationships with two or more of these freaks!

It's easy to half-step and ration your orgasms when cheating. The explanation of being tired from work or some other lame excuse will fly when you're creeping over to the side chick's apartment for a quickie once a week, but being in a transparent relationship where you have sexual responsibilities to two or more women is more than most men can handle. I often hear guys talking about being poly and handling two or more women. I just think to myself, Man, please, go sit down somewhere! And judging by the condition of most of the men I see over fifty, they might mess around and have a heart attack if they can get it up at all!

I wrote a commentary about my interviews with some women in my Facebook poly group on this topic. And their attitude was women have more incentive to be poly than men. In fact, most of them said the idea of sharing a man with another woman was ridiculous, if not laughable.

The whole idea behind polyamory is to share your partner intimately with another person, and in the case of my post, men having multiple women. Not only does that go against most women's morals and religious beliefs, but it also goes against their common sense when their basic needs aren't being met. And that's something that poly women, or women who might be open to poly, won't tolerate!

In my Facebook group, Michael Baisden Poly Lifestyles, I asked my female members to post if they preferred a relationship dynamic that was FMF (Female, Male, Female) or an MFM (Male, Female, Male). In 80% of the cases, they choose MFM. I was shocked the number was so high! But when I reached out to some of them to get an understanding of why they made this choice, they had a similar response: "You can't get half of what you need from one man; sexually, conversationally, and financially, consistency, maturity, and someone you can learn something from!" they said. "Why would I settle for just one?" I was like, "Damn, you can't argue with that!"

■ ■ ■

These women were crystal clear that they had no interest or motivation in sharing their man. On the contrary, they believed that they were the ones who needed an additional partner just to keep things interesting. One of the comments that stood out was from a woman named Maxine. Her words perfectly summarized my point.

Maxine wrote:

Yes, women lose a lot more than men when they get married! When a woman gets married, she cuts off all of her male resources. Men are more likely to help when you are single. Discount or free items women miss out on!

1. *Business advice*
2. *Car repairs*
3. *Yard work*
4. *Movers*
5. *Home maintenance*
6. *Mortgage/rent payments*
7. *Different experiences/sources of entertainment*
8. *Friendships*
9. *Trips*
10. *Dinners*

Nowadays we women are sacrificing a lot! It's like would you rather have one source of income or 7? No one is saying one man can't provide all those things but it's a cap since y'all are now the ones in a marriage. Yes, you can get business advice from your husband, but it's limited. Now if I go to 7 different men I'm getting 7 different views, 7 different experience levels, and 7 different mentors. And if was a single lady, as opposed to being married, my time with these men isn't capped by the responsibilities I have at home as a married woman.

■ ■ ■

Yeah, she said that, and I agree! Interestingly, the same ladies who preferred MFM poly relationships also said they were open to their men having other partners—in fact, they insisted! And this is where the differences between poly men and poly women are so striking. The men almost demanded their partners to be exclusive to them, while the women were open to their men seeing whoever they wanted. And they weren't particularly concerned about being the priority in their male partner's lives. In fact, most of them didn't want the responsibility of being labeled "His woman!" I think more women would be open to poly life if having another man was at least on the table. In their minds, the double standard is unfair, and it's turning them off.

Many women have responsibilities at home, like managing their children and sick parents, or they're grinding in their careers and running their businesses. It makes sense for many of them not to have a man relying on them 100% for dates, phone conversations, and sex. They just want a partner who will be available when they need him.

Fortunately, there are experienced poly men out there who are secure enough not to need to leverage women by using double standards. Mature poly men want peace, too, as well as a clear understanding of what the agreements are in the relationship.

Personally, I don't believe in double standards, rules, or even boundaries, at least not ones that make anyone feel restricted. I believe in being authentic about who I am, communicating my vision for my relationship, and then compromising where I am comfortable, so everyone involved has their needs met. Once that's been established, my attitude toward my partner is, "Do whatever you want to do!" Just make sure I'm the first to know when you want to change something in the relationship that we didn't agree to.

When men hear me say this, they ask, "So, what are the rules, and what's stopping her from having sex with other men?" And that's the disconnect with most guys when it comes to understanding polyamory. My goal is not to control my partners' vaginas or emotions but to set them free. Maintaining order and respect only happens when two people value their relationship enough not to damage it. And that's established based on the information they provide each other from the beginning and throughout the relationship, as well as the honest communication and transparency that's demonstrated consistently. It's that simple!

If your agreement with your woman is to be exclusive, then why worry about what else she's doing with other men? Either you trust her, or you don't! And if you agree that you both can have other partners, then it's up to both of you to agree on the standards of the relationship. I prefer the word "standards" to "rules" because people's feelings change, and I don't want my partner to feel restricted and unable to live freely and talk to me when there is a shift. That's where the lies and omissions begin and when the damage is done.

Most people will never understand the value of this kind of freedom until they meet someone whose company they enjoy or until they fall in love with someone else. When you try to explain this concept to most people, they get defensive. But the truth is, you never know when a person will come along that moves you in a unique way, whether sexual or non-sexual. Living a poly life allows you to pursue those feelings without guilt.

So, let me ask you, have you ever been involved with someone you loved and then met someone you couldn't stop thinking about? Not just in a sexual way but someone you wished you could have in your life as another partner? Many people have, but they dismissed it or suppressed it because they felt guilty. For some, the fact that they're thinking about it makes them feel like a cheater, which is ridiculous. Having a desire for other people is normal, and so is fantasizing about them.

Well, in the poly lifestyle, you can have both partners, whether two men or two women! It's called being in a throuple. The word is a portmanteau or combination of "three-person" and "couple." It's a form of polyamory where three partners are in a relationship with one another.

Throuples can be established by one person bringing two of his partners together or a couple adding another partner. As I mentioned in the previous chapter, adding another partner can spice things up between a couple that still loves each other. Or maybe there's something missing that the new partner adds to the relationship. Those qualities can impact each partner in profoundly different ways. The female might feel heightened sexual energy, whereas the male could find his new female partner a valuable muse passionate about his artistic endeavors. As I said, it's not all about sex.

Throuples also can take on various forms. Some throuples consider themselves in an "Open Triad" where the three people are in a committed relationship with one another while still having the option to date and have sex with other people. Or the three of them may date and play with other individuals or couples. On the other hand, a closed triad is basically a monogamous relationship with three people. No one dates other people or has sexual intercourse outside their two partners.

Lastly, there's the V dynamic of polyamory, where one person is involved with two others, but those two are not involved romantically. This is one of the more common poly dynamics, especially when neither of the partners is bisexual nor necessarily interested in being involved socially with the other person. For the record, the person involved with each set of people is called the "hinge partner!"

This all sounds like fun, right? Well, it can be if everyone involved is transparent about their intentions and communicates when there's a problem, not allowing it to fester. But if they're not being open and honest, you could find yourself in poly situations that can waste your valuable time or become a living hell!

THE CHALLENGES OF POLYAMORY

Having been in many poly situations, there's always one issue that kills the fun and ruins the opportunity for the poly relationship to evolve into something special. And it's not jealousy—it's faking being poly! When someone loves you or has ulterior motives, they often lie about being able to function in a poly relationship.

Poly life is challenging enough without adding deception into the mix. I've heard stories and had my own experiences with women pretending to be poly to hold on to the man. They knew that once they demonstrated they weren't down with the poly life, the relationship would come to an end. But instead of being transparent, they play a role until, eventually, that moment comes when they snap under the pressure of their pretentiousness. And it usually happens sooner rather than later.

Poly life reveals things about you that wouldn't otherwise be revealed. It brings out your insecurities in ways you can't imagine. And it exposes your shortcomings, whether physical, sexual, emotional, or psychological, in how you execute or your lack of execution. That's because there are so many people watching you—up close! You may get away with lying or being inconsistent with one woman or man, but when you're involved in a relationship with multiple people, the jig is up!

And your insecurities are exposed as a man when you are faced with another man being in the picture. For example, in a triad dynamic where there are two heterosexual men involved with one woman, Man One knows his woman is getting tossed by Man Two because great sex is their thing! Add that Man Two earns more money. We all know Man One is going to be trippin'. But Man Two is insecure because Man One spends more time with her, and they may have a child together. Both men love her, and she loves both of them, but even though they have things that bind them, it still doesn't make it easy.

Feelings you never knew you had as a man can surface when faced with unfamiliar situations with a woman you love. And it doesn't even have to be another man involved. Sometimes, simply sharing fantasies can be too much for some men to handle—let alone the real thing!

And the same kinds of insecurities can creep into a

woman's mind when another female comes onto the scene. The other woman might be younger, have a tighter body, or she's just new! Sometimes, that's enough to bring out a woman's insecurities! Whether it's a situation where the man brings the two women together or a couple chooses to add her to their relationship, it's only natural for jealousy and women's competitive nature to kick in. This happens with not all women but most. And that's just the beginning of the problems if the primary couple doesn't have a strong and transparent relationship. Things can get messy real quick!

All of us probably know at least one woman who's been invited into a throuple and then had it go terribly wrong! Most often, the husband or boyfriend gets caught up, falls in love with her, and loses interest in his wife or girlfriend. Or the wife or girlfriend falls in love with her and wants to leave the husband so they can run off together. I think it's the man's responsibility to ensure his relationship is solid before bringing another woman into his home and bed. Too many men get frantic over the idea of having two women sexually and do the work it takes to introduce both women into a stable situation.

And that's the most annoying aspect of trying to live the poly life. There are too many disingenuous and half-steppin' people going at it in the wrong way. Couples use outsiders to try to fix their problems with intimacy instead of doing the work as a couple first. And too many people are pretending to be poly to satisfy the other partner's desires. Usually, it's the wife or girlfriend putting up with another woman being in her bed so the man can live out his fantasies and not leave her. They're not being poly; that's being messy, and the result is always disastrous!

Meanwhile, the unicorn, meaning the woman brought into the relationship to satisfy the couple, is pissed off because she thought she had a good thing and has to start all over again! She's lost the man she loved and a woman who was a good friend and a great lover. And often, there are children involved who she has to detach from emotionally, making the experience all the more painful.

I guess it's human nature to ruin a good thing! Sometimes, no matter how transparent and upfront you are about being poly, they'll always be people who fuck it up! They can't stop lying about who they are, whether it's their relationship status or what their intentions are! So, a word of advice: if you want to stay ahead of the game in this poly life, constantly be on the lookout for poly perpetrators!

■ ■ ■

Jealousy is a major challenge when you're polyamorous! And sadly, people accept jealousy and being territorial as something natural and impossible to resolve. And to be fair, some people can't get past it. Hell, I have some jealous feelings that spring up every now and then, and I have to check myself! But faced with the choice between having someone extraordinary in your life and having them leave, wouldn't it be wise to figure it out?

Like any other non-productive personality trait like impatience, procrastination, being judgmental, or being close-minded, jealousy can and should be worked out. It can destroy important parts of your life because it's rooted in insecurity, which ruins everything!

Insecurity is defined *as a feeling of inadequacy (not being good enough) and uncertainty. It produces anxiety about your goals, relationships, and ability to handle certain situations.*

Being jealous and territorial isn't something that we should accept as unfixable. Yes, it's natural to feel jealousy, but it's unintelligent to allow it to control you. It's no wonder jealousy and insecurity are the main causes of poly relationships failing, and I'm sure it's the reason for many monogamous relationships ending as well.

To be fair, I think we can contribute to our partner's insecurities by acting inappropriately and being inconsistent. And there's more of an opportunity for that kind of bad behavior in the poly life because having attractive people in your spaces is a part of the lifestyle. But just because other people are welcome doesn't mean overstepping boundaries is okay. Either play by the rules, or don't play at all! Some examples of bad poly experiences were posted by members of my poly group on Facebook! Pay close attention to the last story! It's a doozie!

Kim wrote:
I don't think everyone was faking. I think people believed they could handle the dynamics, and their feelings got caught up. People really believe they can control every emotion all the time. As we can see, it's not possible. We're binding into relationships with intentions to suppress certain feelings, then boom. 1 conversation, 1 dinner, 1 kiss or 1 pleasure move later has us second guessing those intentions. How u feel today, may not be how u feel tomorrow.

Tai wrote:
I was introduced to a couple that dated separately. When he and I began to get close the wife's insecurities began to appear. All of us would have frequent dates at their house but the energy became weird. We're good friends but I chose not to be involved beyond that.

Joy wrote:
When I dated couples in the early 2 K's, I always spent alone time with each partner. The women always said they were together, but the men would always say they were just friends. I was single so I smashed whomever I was having the best time with. 👻

KL wrote:
My partner and I were initially cool with the idea of bringing in another female. It was agreed that everyone would contribute equally, and no one was bigger than the dynamic.

Well, that went right out the window. My partner and the other woman didn't follow the boundaries that we all agreed to in regard to how much time and attention would be given to each person. It came to a head about two weeks ago. They began to act as a duo and made me feel like an outsider. I told them, "This isn't what we agreed to!" He responded by telling me to leave, and she was obviously cool with it because she didn't speak up. Now they are a couple.

So, I'm now baffled! Did he just use me to get with this female? Afterall, he was the one who entertained the idea of adding someone into our relationship and bedroom in the first place. Now that I'm single again I don't know if I want to even indulge in the lifestyle again. It was nice while it lasted but how do you really know if someone is truly down with the dynamic or just using you? I'm open to monogamy and poly I just need a man who's going to be honest and transparent with me!

■ ■ ■

Transparency is the biggest challenge in any relationship, especially in polyamory ones. We're not trained to be open about being sexually attracted to others. And we're certainly not taught that it's okay to share with our partners that we love someone else. Instead of doing poly the right way, we use people authentically interested in the lifestyle just to have sex with other people. KL's story is more common than you think. People will introduce the idea of polyamory, and once the second person comes into the relationship, they dump the primary partner for the "new piece." That's not being poly; that's being a jerk!

Almost everyone new to poly life struggles with the newness of it. The idea of putting your sexual desires and emotional needs on the table is foreign to all of us. Traditional marriage has had centuries to improve, and it hasn't. In fact, it's gotten worse. Not because the institution is flawed but because people are. And, let's be honest, poly life is new, unsupported by society, and hard as hell to pull off.

Does that mean you give up on it? Of course, not! But anyone who pursues this love style should be prepared to be rejected, judged, and encounter a lot of wannabes who don't know what the hell they're doing. There are simply not enough experienced people to educate others about the right way to be poly. This book is my attempt to clear up some ambiguities and encourage people not to give up. Anything that adds value to your life is worth fighting for!

POLY DOESN'T HAVE TO BE FOREVER

I laugh at the reaction I get from people when I share with them that I'm poly. Many of them respond as if I need an intervention—like it's some kind of cult I need to be rescued from. Polyamory isn't a lifetime prison sentence. You don't have to be poly forever! Many people flow in and out of polyamory just as individuals flow in and out of marriage, dating, or having casual sex. Living as a poly couple or solo poly person is often a choice at that moment, with a particular person to explore, or during a certain chapter of your life.

Choosing to be polyamorous isn't a pledge to a cult that you can't escape from. There's no intervention required to become monogamous again. Sometimes, it's all a matter of who's in your life. I mean, you can't be poly by yourself, and you can't be poly with a partner who isn't open to it. And to be honest, sometimes you need a break from dealing with multiple people.

That's why I think it's important to share with potential partners that you're a poly person who happens to be single at that moment. I'm not sure you can even promise someone that you'll never be poly again in the same way I would never say never to marriage. Do I need it or fantasize about marriage? No! But could I say I would never do it again? Of course not! I'm not anti-marriage, just as I'm not anti-monogamy. But

I think it's only fair to know a person's lifestyle history and preferences before you get in too deep. Then, if they choose to continue to be intimate with you, at least you know you've been transparent.

I know that people say they are non-monogamous by nature, but I think if you're intelligent, you adapt to who is in your life and make the necessary compromises. It's possible you could be happy in a long-term monogamous relationship. The key, I believe, is not to promise to be monogamous but to promise to communicate when you decide not to be so that your partner has a choice to stay or leave.

Imagine your partner having sex with another person. Now imagine them enjoying it to the point of moaning and screaming in ecstasy. For some people, that vision isn't a turn-on; it's their worst nightmare. For others, it's just another Friday night!

But regardless of how you feel about Swinging, you have to admire couples that are secure enough to allow their partner to live out their fantasies by having sex with others and doing it out in the open, with no lies, no closed doors, and no holding back!

That's Why I Love Swingers!

16

WHY I LOVE SWINGERS!

Have you ever been to a swinger's club? I have many times, and those were some of the best parties I've ever been to. My first experience was back in the early 2000s. A business associate of mine and her husband used to swing when they were married. But she stopped going to the club after they divorced. One day while we were having drinks and shooting the breeze at my home in Miami with a couple of my lady friends, she invited us to check out a swinger's club in Ft. Lauderdale called Trapeze.

I'm not going to lie; I was apprehensive. All kinds of visions swirled in my head of White people walking around naked and having sex all over the place. But my associate, an exotic Latina, painted a picture of a classy place where I would be in the company of sophisticated couples and mature adults just out to have a good time. It helped that she was well-educated and a successful business owner. I knew she valued her reputation as much as I did mine. So, I said, "What the hell, let's do this!" And my two lady friends who were visiting from out of town were just as excited to check it out!

We arrived at the club around eleven. The parking lot was half empty, and I was glad the crowd hadn't arrived yet. I needed time to get acclimated to the environment and to knock down a couple of drinks to loosen up! I can't recall what the cover was to get in, but I remember the price was high enough to keep riff-raff out. That made me feel more comfortable.

Saturday night was couple's night, which meant men were not allowed into the club without being accompanied by a female. That was another factor that made me and my guests feel more at ease. Having a bunch of horny uncoupled men hoovering around would not have been a good first experience. Single women, of course, are always welcome in swinger's clubs. In fact, women control that whole environment.

One of the biggest misconceptions about swinging is that men coerce women into the lifestyle. And that may be true in some cases. But authentic swing clubs are places where powerful and sexually confident females can feel safe to express themselves. They don't need a man's validation. They openly choose this life—they crave it!

I think people would be surprised by how many men are introduced to swinging by women and not the other way around. The truth is most men have no idea what their woman is down for because they either haven't presented it to her the right way or they haven't established the trust and consistency that demonstrates to a woman that he can handle it. Anyway, let me return to my virgin experience at the swinger's club.

After paying the fee to get in, I checked my two bottles of wine and a large bottle of Grey Goose. They attached stickers to the bottles and handed me a laminated card with a number. For those who've never been to a swinger's club, the establishment is not allowed to sell alcohol. You have to bring your own liquor, and the bartender will serve you. At least, that's how it worked back in the day!

Once we found a spot at the bar with a view of the dance floor, we settled in and ordered drinks. The atmosphere was nice, and the music was banging! People boast about how great the music is at strip clubs, but some of the best DJs I have ever heard were at swingers clubs. There was a DJ who used to spin at a Dallas swinger's club that was so good I hired him to create mixes for my national radio show. Shout out to you, DJ Lamb, one of the *baddest* White boys to ever spin on my radio show!

Sorry, I keep digressing, but writing about my swing club experiences reminds me of many fun and exciting times. So, where was I?

By midnight, the crowd began to grow. And just as my Latina associate told me, there were many attractive couples, the vast majority over forty. They were dressed classy in suits and nice dresses. It wasn't at all like I expected. The crowd was mostly White, but there were some Blacks and Hispanics in the mix. Everyone was cordial, saying hello and welcoming us to the club. Surprisingly many of them were also there for the first time or had recently joined. They made us feel right at home.

As the night went on, the crowd grew thicker and louder! The drinks were flowing, and the music got even better. By 1:00 am, the party was jumping. Some of the ladies began to take off their tops, some went completely naked, and a group of them took to the dance floor and began dancing in a circle next to the mirrored wall. My two lady friends and the ladies with their husbands standing next to us joined in the fun!

If you've ever been to a swingers club, you know it's the ladies who get the party started! Women are the ones who initiate approaching other women. And it's the women who decide which couples they're attracted to. The other guys and I sat back in the cut, having drinks and watching the show. It was a high like I've experienced! And so much fun! But while all this was happening, I knew there was more to come, and I couldn't wait to experience it!

Eventually, people began to disappear into the back rooms. Being the curious and adventurous person I am, I grabbed my friends, and we went to check it out. Now, I'm not going to get into the particulars of what went down 'cause that ain't none of y'all's business. But I will say that everything that we saw in the back room was consensual, sanitary, and handled responsibly, whether it was in the hot tubs, sofa area, or the sex room that was lined with mattresses. After that night, I never looked at swingers or swing clubs the same.

What stood out that night, as well as my other experiences at swing clubs, was how many years most of the couples had been together. Nearly all of them had been together for seven or more years, many over fifteen. They all seemed happy—and they looked damn good!

I think that's important to highlight because swingers are often portrayed as sexual caricatures with no loyalties or conscious. When in fact, they are mostly couples who have been through a lot together, raised families, are well educated, accomplished, and have decided that instead of throwing away a great partnership, they would rather explore their sexual fantasies together. And that's why I love swingers; they have invested years into their relationships, love their partners, and trust them enough to share them sexually if that makes their partners happy.

For some people, that concept sounds crazy! Many have said to me, "How can you love someone and be okay with them having sex with other people?" I get it because I used to feel the same way! Yes, I love swingers, but I haven't swung! I've been open to sharing my partners if that's what they want, but I haven't had to do it—yet! And if and when it happens, I have no doubt that it will present a challenge. Fantasizing about your woman being stroked by a man who's really into her, and she's into him, is different than actually seeing it go down in front of you.

As I said, I get it! And those who swing would be the first to tell you, "This lifestyle isn't for everyone!" And they're right! I've been around swingers for decades and produced two documentaries about sex and relationships that featured swingers. This lifestyle has all kinds of stories: the good, the bad, and the ugly. The good is when relationships are elevated to new heights, and the couples learn more about themselves and each other. The wife, who the husband thought was boring and cold, erupts into a passionate sex machine, and suddenly, their mundane relationship becomes something fun and exciting again!

But swinging could also be the worst decision you ever made, especially if you're trying to fix a broken relationship or rekindle passions that are dead as a doornail. Swinging is designed to enhance your partnership, not a cure for problems that have been dormant and festering for years. Suppose you're looking for a substitute for your partner. Then you need to split up and do your own thing. There are plenty of men and women who are solo swingers, just as there are those who are solo poly. Don't force swinging onto your partner, pretending you're using it to spice things up so you can stay together when what you've really done is look for a replacement. The decision to swing should aim to create a new and exciting beginning for both of you.

It's hard enough to be successful at swinging when you have a relationship that's solid. But if you don't have good intentions or don't do the work before swinging, it can turn into a complete train wreck!

Ladies, imagine how you would feel watching your man giving a woman head at a swinger's party like he's been starving for it, and you're feeling "some kind of way" because he never goes down on you. And his reaction is over the top after penetrating her with excessive moaning and pounding her as if he hasn't been satisfied in ages. And to cap off, he kisses her passionately on the lips, even though you both agreed that kissing was overstepping the boundaries.

This is not the sign of a couple enjoying playing together but a man out to get his! And couples experienced in Swinging can see right through these unstable relationships because they've seen it many times before where one or both partners are swinging, hoping they can hide from the other just to get their freak on! It's awkward for everybody, and it's not what the lifestyle is about.

And it's just as awkward and disruptive to a swinger's party when the woman is being inappropriate and breaking the rules. Some women come into these parties on the rebound from bad or abusive marriages or relationships—motivated by their partner's inconsistencies and sloppy conduct with other females! Or she could simply be trifling and looking to get her fuck on! Regardless of her mindset, the last place you want to be as a couple or single female is at a swinger's party with a bunch of unresolved emotional issues!

I've seen women go rogue at swinger's parties, and it traumatizes their partners. There was an incident at a Dallas swinger's club I'll never forget. I was a regular there for a few months. One Saturday night, a White couple that I hadn't seen before showed up. From the jump, you could tell by the way they interacted separately from one another that their situation wasn't solid. When you're new to a swinger's club, other swingers are watching the way you move, trust me!

I was told by one of the waitresses who had become friendly with that the couple had been regulars but had disappeared for a while. Maybe one of them talked the other into revisiting the lifestyle, but it was clear after the party got crackin' that they weren't on the same page.

The wife began flirting with a lot of the Black men who were there with their partners. She seemed very familiar with many of the people who were sitting in the corner, and that's where many of the regulars would congregate. It was clear from her level of affection towards the women that they had a history. At first, the boyfriend seemed cool with all the flirtation that was going on with the Black men, which excluded him. But as the night went on, he became noticeably irritated, especially after she took off for the private area upstairs with two Black couples trailing her. A few minutes later, he went upstairs after her. My partner and I, being nosey, went up too. This was turning into a real-life swinger's drama, and I wasn't about to miss it!

By the time we made it upstairs, they had this White woman in a chair orgy that Caligula would have been proud of. She was naked, sitting on her knees, doggy style, over an oversized black leather chair with one of the Black women underneath her sucking her breast while one of the Black men was penetrating her from behind. The other Black woman was slapping her on the ass while kissing her man, who was stroking her hair. And just as we could get a clear view, we could see the second Black man making his way to get in front of her. He pulled out his dick, slid a condom on, and put it in her mouth. I've never heard a woman moan and whine like that before. They were tearing her ass up, and she loved it!

Now, I know you're asking yourselves, "Where was her man while all of this was happening?" Well, he was sitting opposite them on a matching black leather chair, acting like he was enjoying it. I say "acting" because I could see the pain and humiliation on his face. He tried to play it off like it was "all good," but it was tearing him up inside. He was drunk but fully aware that his woman was putting on a show— and it was making him look weak!

Men should know better than to bring an unhappy woman into a swinging environment, especially one who has felt unappreciated and is unfulfilled sexually. Men naively believe that being a swinger is all to their benefit, but let me assure you that swinging is a female-dominated world! What a man can do in the swinging life, a woman can do ten times better and nastier. So, be careful what you ask for when you say you want to swing! It's not just the physicality of having sex that can trigger a person but watching your partner reach emotional depths and orgasmic heights that you've never seen them reach before.

Whether it's due to an interaction with someone of the opposite sex or the same sex, it can change how you look at your partner forever! For those who aren't built for swinging, it can be dramatizing and destroy your relationship. But for those who know what it means to have compersion, each stroke and satisfying moan is beautiful!

So, what is compersion? According to the website www. whatiscompersion.com, compersion is defined as whole-heartedly participating in the happiness of your partner. It is the sympathetic joy you feel for somebody else, even when their positive experience doesn't involve or benefit you directly. Thus, compersion can be thought of as the opposite of jealousy and possessiveness!

I realize that this concept is hard to understand since people have a difficult time allowing their partners to love their friends, family members, and even their own children, so you know most people can't imagine their partners being loved, catered to, touched, and sexually satisfied by someone of the opposite sex, or even pleasured by someone of the same sex.

To be honest, I often question whether I could genuinely experience compersion with a partner. It's easy to say what you're open to until you experience it. I'm accustomed to men being attracted to my female partners when we are out in public, even approaching them at my events, but I've never been in a situation where my partner was being kissed, licked on, and penetrated by another man in my presence.

Am I still open to it? Sure, if that's the understanding going into the relationship! And even if our relationship dynamic was poly with only female partners, I would be open to exploring if our relationship was on solid ground. I feel it's my duty to satisfy my partner's desires and fantasies. And I would hope she feels the same. Besides, I'm sexually adventurous, so it's not really a stretch! In the past, I've been the one to initiate the idea of playing with other couples, but my partners weren't open to it, and if there's one thing you learn in any type of relationship, it is not to force things on your partner! It never turns out well!

I posted the question about compersion to my followers. As usual, they had some interesting and educational responses. Now to be clear, neither they nor I believe swinging is the answer for every couple, but it has helped many of them re-invent and renew their relationships! But for swinging to enhance your partnership, you must be honest about whether this is what you both truly want, and it's not one person talking the other into it. A word to the wise, if you don't have the same intention, if you can't stay within the boundaries you set, and if you don't have compersion, you'll swing right into a disaster.

Here's what experienced swingers had to say about their compersion and the challenges of this lifestyle. Take notes!

Ella wrote:
During "her turn" I'm usually doing something with another guy or jump into the mix with them. It's always fun to watch but ultimately, it's a group activity. I love doing things with them to enhance their time. I love doing things to him to put him over the edge with her. It's like a sexy game. And, oh, don't forget, you can learn more about your partner during that time, too...and yourself. New things you can try together later, etc.

Althyia wrote:
Watching him break her back is a turn on...then I look at her and say "now you understand why I smile so much!!"

De Shaw wrote:
Not watching watching cuz I'll be putting in work with the wife or girlfriend of the guy that's doing her but the sounds of her being satisfied is music to my ears.

Jeanine wrote:
Their pleasure is the turn on. Knowing their partner is happy. I know it sounds difficult to understand. It's not for everybody.

Shawnana wrote:
I'm not usually watching. I'm much more into what's happening to me. But I love hearing the moans and smacks and all the stuff!!! It's play time! We're all there to have fun!

James wrote:
Truthfully most people are aroused visually. It was very erotic and very arousing for me and her at the time, as we both enjoyed threesomes together. It takes a very secure partner, which I am, and my partner at the time was as well. Her pleasure was my pleasure, so it was great for both of us.

LaQuitta wrote:
I'm his cheerleader, get that, give it to her, yessssssssssssss baby, handle that!! U like it, tell her! Yeah, I'm all into it. His pleasure is our pleasure.

Summer Neal wrote:
I enjoy it! It's one of the biggest turn-ons to see my man pleasing another woman.

Richard wrote:
I enjoy seeing my woman pleased by another man, but I'm not cool with him handling her any kind of way. There has to be respect and boundaries. You have to be able to trust that your partner is going to respect herself and make sure the man is respecting her as well and respecting your relationship.

I've seen dudes come into these parties just looking to smash with no regard for safety protocols or boundaries. Fights have broken out at some parties because people don't know how to act. That's why it's up to you and your partner to check each other and the people you get with.

*I don't care how well endowered he is because I'm packing
a big one too, but don't start talking shit to my woman like,
"Who's pussy is it?" Calling her a bitch and whispering in
her ear trying to be slick. That will shut my woman down
instantly and you might get punched in the mf face! Because
everyone is told the rules in advance!*

*Also, people need to always use protection and understand
the emotional risk. If you're swinging on a regular basis
with the same people, feelings can get involved and some
people become addicted. No, it shouldn't happen, but that's a
chance you take!*

■ ■ ■

I agree with Richard; there are serious risks in swinging.
STIs should be a real concern, and protection should always
be mandatory. But swingers, at least, aren't lying about being
monogamous, which is where most of the transmission is
coming from. And swingers are open about having sex with
other people, and their partner knows who those people
are. Hell, they're probably in the same room together or at
least under the same roof. Again, that's why I love swingers,
because of their transparency.

Personally, I don't think you can trust anyone hundred
percent, whether you're swinging or in a monogamous relationship. And I always tell women I'm involved with that I
will never trust them 100% with everything!

But what I do need to trust is your priorities to put us
first. I need to trust your judgment to protect my health and
not humiliate me. And most importantly, I have to trust that
you will communicate with me when things shift in how you

feel about me to give me a chance to talk about it or to leave. No one should take away your choice with a lie or omission.

That's why I'm passionate about transparency, and I want you to insist on it too. Stop allowing people to operate in grey areas, start valuing your time, and tell them, better yet, warn them—from day one, "Don't Lie To Me!"

Now that I've gotten that off my chest—Swing On!

START LIVING
WITH INTENTION

The last section of this book is dedicated to those who have the audacity to think outside the box and to change!

I know change is hard! Culture, religion, and upbringing are powerful influences. But change is possible once you reach a point of utter frustration, complete failure, or excruciating pain!

Some people refer to this as their "Aha" moment. It's that moment you recognize that your life will remain stagnant until you start living with a sense of urgency! That's when you stop caring about what others think and start going after what you want—relentlessly!

So, here's to everyone ready to be transparent with themselves and take responsibility for creating their own happiness and peace!

17

DON'T DISTURB
THIS GROOVE

Once you create a peaceful life, you better protect it like it's the most precious thing on Earth. Most people spend their entire adult lives working to be free of debt, free of their children's presence in their homes, and free of controlling partners—basically freeing themselves of stress and worry. So, when someone comes along offering love, a mature person responds, "Does that love include peace and quiet? Because if it doesn't, you can go take a flying leap!"

I'm not saying love isn't important, but love alone doesn't cut it for those who've experienced what damage blind love can cause. We've all been in love, fallen in love, and searched for love, only to find it and discover that, too often, love comes with drama, unstainable compromises, hidden agendas, financial costs, and emotional and physical abuse.

So, while love is always welcome, it's not a priority for mature men and women who need more than an emotional high. What we're searching for isn't more love but more peace. And because many of us have worked so hard to create peaceful lives, we are apprehensive about inviting just anybody into our tranquil spaces!

I know that sounds selfish, but having peace of mind and peace within your living space isn't easy to create and even harder to sustain. You've got to have a plan for it, cultivate it, and then protect it from those who aren't accustomed to living in a peaceful place. People tend to romanticize relationships by telling you that all you need is love, but we know that's nonsense! Love doesn't make you compatible with someone who watches television with the volume jacked up. Love doesn't make it easier to tolerate a partner who likes to entertain many friends and family in the home you share. And love can't make you ignore someone who is sloppy or insist on decorating in a way that throws off your energy.

These issues may sound petty to some, but those of us who are into vibes and energy know that the wrong furniture, paintings, plants, animals, and floor coverings can influence your vibration. Even lighting matters; whether it's the amount of sunlight that's allowed into a room or the lighting levels on your faders, it all matters. Being compatible is about more than finances, personalities, emotions, and sex. To me, it's more about how you think, what you believe, how you eat, and what kind of vibe you come home to!

Just finding a quiet place to live can take years! It's nearly impossible to find a place where noisy neighbors, barking dogs, or endless construction do not stress you out. And if you live in an apartment building, you're rolling the dice each time you sign a lease!

If you have people living above you, chances are they'll drive you crazy, stomping around all hours of the day and night. We've all had those loud ass neighbors who push us to the point of banging a broom on the ceiling and yelling, "Stop all that damned stomping and sit your asses down somewhere!"

So, while love makes you feel all warm and fuzzy, it doesn't make up for the years it takes to produce a peaceful life. Therefore, it doesn't matter how great the sex is, how attractive they are, or how much money they're bringing to the table. If they disturb the groove, they're going to be handed their coat and politely escorted out!

Yes, I'm speaking from experience. And yes, I kicked her out without bothering to explain why the date was being cut short. Like many of you, I always make it clear when I'm getting acquainted with someone that my peace is everything! And I made it clear to this person before I extended the invitation. So, once she started giving off negative energy by talking loudly, name-dropping, and cursing way too much, I stood up and gestured toward the door. "Look, I'm going to get back to work." I opened the door and gave her a cordial hug. "Thanks for stopping by." I shut the door behind her, lit a joint, poured myself a tall glass of wine, and got back into my groove.

SET IN YOUR WAYS

By the time people reach their mid-thirties, they're already set in their ways of doing things, especially people who have never lived with anyone. Even if you're single with children, you become set in the ways your house functions. By 40, you've gotten "real" comfortable with your processes and routines. And by fifty, forget about it! You've grown accustomed to the thermostats being set at a certain temperature, the kitchen being closed by nine, and being in bed by ten—with the ceiling fan on! You're deep into your groove, and nothing can disturb it!

Now, that's not to say people aren't open to compromise if a worthy person comes along. But let's keep it real; how long can a relationship survive if the objective is to live together when you've been alone for years or even spending extended weekends in the same space? Loving someone and living with them are two entirely different things.

The title of this book, *Don't Lie To Me,* isn't just about being honest with your partners about cheating but about being honest with yourself about what you can tolerate regardless of the circumstances. People like to think they can be flexible for the right person, but adapting to having people in your space is challenging, especially after you reach a certain age or if you've been alone for years, if not decades.

Just look at cohabitating from a historical perspective. There's no precedence for the millions of people who find themselves single over forty, fifty, and sixty living comfortably in their own space. It has nothing to do with being selfish. We simply live in a time when older people have the financial means to live comfortably in their space. Many single people have retired well, and the idea of giving up those comforts for the sake of not being alone doesn't move them, especially if they've tried and failed before.

I realize it's difficult to find a quality partner, but it

can be even harder to regain your peace once you allow someone in who throws everything off! Human beings tend to bring chaos into serene spaces. They lie, deceive, and become lazy and inconsistent once they get their foot in the door. Yes, love and relationships are important. No one wants to grow old alone. Still, we should also be mindful that with every new relationship comes the risk of losing your peace of mind, your peace and quiet, and inviting uncertainty into your home, all in the name of compromising—but compromising what?

COMPROMISE FOR WHAT?

I live my life with one objective, and that is to be happy! Every decision I make professionally, financially, and in my intimate relationships is measured against how it will affect how good I feel about myself and my life when I wake up every morning. I live with the intention of being happy! Not to be in love, rich, or sexually gratified—my mission is happiness!

Like many of you, I'm of a certain age, and I've already made sacrifices for my daughter, family, career, employees, and partners. And for the right person, I'm willing to cooperate to make our relationship work for both of us. But I'm at a point where I'm not so sure I'm willing to compromise.

The word "compromise" has been used so casually that it's unclear to me what the actual meaning is when applied to modern-day relationships. So, for the sake of not being presumptuous, I think we should start talking in specifics as to what that expectation of compromise is. And this is especially critical for women since, if we're being real, they are the ones who are usually the ones being asked to compromise. In my experience, people who expect compromise often do so to create a more manageable, tolerable, or controllable version of you instead of accepting you for who you are.

Before writing this chapter, I watched a YouTube video of an interview with the late actress Eartha Kitt. She was speaking on the topic of compromise. I highly recommend you watch it. In fact, watch as many interviews of this dynamic woman as you can find. She lived an extraordinary life, and she's a deep thinker.

During the interview, she was asked, "Can anyone live with Eartha Kitt?" She replied, "That's not for me to decide. That's for someone who decides to live with me to decide—not for me."

Then the reporter asked her, "But are you willing to compromise within the relationship?" Eartha Kitt turned toward him and stared intensely into the camera. "Compromise?" she responded, sounding agitated. "What is compromising? Compromising for what?" she went on. "Compromising for what reason? What is compromise?" she asked him.

"If a man came into your life, wouldn't you want to compromise?" the reporter replied.

Eartha suddenly let out a loud and prolonged laugh! And just as suddenly, her expression turned serious. "Stupid!" she said to him. "A man comes into my life, and I have to compromise? You must think about that one again!"

Again, she let out a sarcastic laugh that grew louder. She was clearly offended by his question. She turned toward him and repeated herself. "A man comes into my life, and I have to compromise—for what? A relationship is a relationship that has to be earned, not compromised for."

She went on to say how she loved relationships and how she thought they were fantastic, wonderful, and great! But here's where she dropped a gem. She stared at him and said, "I think there's nothing in the world more beautiful than falling in love." She paused, and as she spoke, her tone became more reflective. "But falling in love for the right reason. Falling in love for the right purpose. When you fall in love, what is there to compromise about?"

The reporter then asked her, "Isn't love a union between two people? Or does Eartha fall in love with herself?"

She took a moment to contemplate, then she replied, "Yes, I fall in love with myself, and I want someone to share it with me." She paused again, looking away from the camera, and then stared back and said in a compassionate tone, "I want someone to share me—with me."

■ ■ ■

I believe most of us live with the intention of being loved and loving someone, but I think we mistakenly view love as an experience to be pursued. And that we must transform ourselves into someone else to attract and deserve it. But after listening to Eartha Kitts's interview, it reaffirms to me that having self-love is where our focus needs to be.

Self-love is a groove! When you possess it, demonstrate it, and exude it, self-love becomes tangible—something you can share with your partner. Just as Eartha spoke about, you can invite them into your world and your groove.

I also agree with Eartha when she demanded an answer to the question, "Compromise for what?" Personally, I've never had to compromise in my relationships. Did I have to adapt to certain things? Absolutely! But adapting comes naturally when you grow into love with a compatible partner—for the right reason and purpose. In the words of Eartha Kitt, "When you fall in love, what is there to compromise about?"

I'm in this new chapter of my life where I have decided to be transparent and honest with everyone I'm dating. I realize some will get it and stay, and others won't. In either case, I'm good. But it took me 58 years of living, confirming, dodging, hiding, crying, and hurting, and I still wasn't happy.

One day I literally said to myself, "I have done it one way, and I didn't get the results I wanted, so let's switch it up!" And honestly, I'm more at peace and the happiest I've ever been. Healing and not giving a f**k does that to a person.

I'm praying for transparency in your book and for those that read it to get healed and set free! ~
— Maria Dominguez

18

TRANSPARENCY SETS YOU FREE

Pursuing a transparent life is one of the most courageous and liberating things you will ever do! Recognizing the importance of self-honesty and self-awareness is essential to becoming transparent. This transformation doesn't happen out loud or all at once. It happens quietly in your thoughts, progresses into actions, and then gradually announces itself to anyone who encounters you. It becomes your mindset and your vibe!

Some compare living transparently to a religious experience, but I try to discourage anyone from making that comparison. Living a transparent life only requires honesty, whereas religion has rules, customs, and restrictions. And religious leaders are given the authority to decide where those boundaries should be. Living transparently is the exact opposite; it says, "Fuck the rules, fuck the norms, and fuck people's expectations—this is who I am, so take it or leave it!"

Until you reach this level of "fuckdome," you'll never be honest with yourself, and, therefore, you'll never be free! And that's where the work of living a transparent life begins; by putting yourself first. Not in a selfish and egotistical way but prioritizing yourself to receive love, not from outsiders but giving love to yourself. And loving yourself is complete when you know who you are.

If you're serious about living a free and transparent life, your journey must include traveling to the country of your ancestors. As someone who has traveled to Africa many times, I can tell you there's a sense of freedom and pride that can only come from knowing and understanding your place in time, your true culture, and your responsibilities to those who came before you.

I've had the opportunity to travel the world and learn more about my history as an African American man, and no trip was more impactful than visiting the slave castles in Ghana. Going to the motherland for the first time and stepping foot on the ground was an emotional experience. Touching the ground inside the cells where thousands of my ancestors were enslaved and where they bled and died was overwhelming!

Those of you who have traveled to your country of origin understand exactly what I'm talking about; learning your history is liberating and empowering. The pride that comes with having a deeper knowledge of self is a kind of freedom that's unexplainable—you have to experience it for yourself. But you don't have to travel overseas to begin your journey. Yours can begin as mine did through reading.

In order to truly learn, you have to free your mind from everything you've been taught. To use a metaphor, you must erase your hard drive and upgrade to new software. Our parents can only project onto us their vision of what they want us to be, and then society works to conform us to fit into its matrix. But learning and ultimately freeing yourself requires more research and some homework.

FREE YOUR MIND

In one of the scenes from the blockbuster movie, *The Matrix*, Neo, played by Keanu Reeves, is given an ultimatum by Morpheus, played by Lawrence Fishburne. "Take the blue pill, and the story ends. You wake in your bed, and you believe what you want to believe. You take the red pill, and you stay in wonderland, and I show you how deep the rabbit hole goes."

My journey down that rabbit hole began as a young man in my mid-twenties, and I've been falling ever since. And like the character Neo, I felt something in my life wasn't right; that I was living in a world that I no longer fit into, at least not comfortably.

Most of you have experienced this too. This is why the Matrix story resonated with so many of us. There is a part of us that feels like we're living in a society designed to control us, or as Morpheus describes in the movie, "a prison for your mind!"

The journey to free your mind is set in motion when you become so utterly frustrated with the state of your life that you know with every fiber of your being that you have to do something—if you truly want to live! And like Neo, you must take that same leap of faith by taking the Red Pill! Living a lie or consciously living an incomplete life, which, as far as I'm concerned, is the same thing, causes a heightened level of anxiety that only those trying to escape the matrix can explain. The truth is most of us sense these subtle vibrations within our world that feel a little off. We start seeing things differently, we become more distant from our stagnant friends, and we begin to feel disconnected from the place where we live, whether it's our old neighborhood, the city we grew up in, or our country— it just stops being enough! And the worst part about facing the reality that you must escape this mental prison is you're all alone trying to break out!

It is the drive to escape, to free our minds, that drives us towards becoming more reclusive and independent, which for most of us leads to the need to start our own businesses. Some of us are natural entrepreneurs, but the majority of people pursue it for one very important reason; it represents freedom! I craved that freedom even as a child. I was the kid selling popcorn and candy from my mother's patio door, setting up lemonade stands, throwing house parties, and charging people to get in. I wasn't just making money; I was taking charge of my life. And I started several businesses over the years because, like many of you, I need to have control to feel at peace!

But the event that brought the matrix into focus and reminded me that I was a slave to my job was one brutally cold winter in my hometown of Chicago while I was driving trains for the Chicago Transit Authority (CTA). I was a flagman on the blue line outside of O'Hare Airport. It was a frigid day in the low twenties outside, but the wind whipping off Lake Michigan made it feel more like zero! They don't call it the Windy City for nothing!

My shift had just ended! I flagged down a train to pick me up off the tracks. When the doors opened, a few passengers gave me a hand. The moment I closed the doors, the bite of just how cold I was hit me! My eyes began to water, and my glasses fogged up! When I took them off to wipe them, I could see a White family standing on the opposite side next to the doors. They had so much luggage it blocked the isles. I vividly remember the image of all of them wearing colorful tropical hats, and most of them were made of straw—the kind you would expect to see on the beach in The Bahamas.

At that moment, I felt like a sucker! There I was, freezing my ass off, working like a slave for an hourly wage, and this man was taking his family on vacation in late December. I don't know why that moment is etched in my mind, but I've never forgotten it or how out of control of my life I felt.

I should be taking my daughter on vacation, I thought to myself. I wanted to get away from that bitter Chicago cold. But what I wanted most was to get the hell away from a job that dictated how much money I earned and when I could go on vacation. From that day forward, I spent every waking moment plotting my escape from the matrix! And the Red Pill, for me, was represented by books!

When someone controls your schedule and the amount of money you earn, they control your life. That's what being an employee of the CTA represented to me. But I decided that if I was going to be physically trapped on those trains, I had to escape mentally. And so, just like in the movie *Shawshank Redemption*, I started to plot my escape and dig my way out one day, one book at a time!

When I was 28 years old, I began my reading journey. Until then, I hadn't read much of anything that wasn't required in school. But once I found a bookstore that catered to my interest called Westside Books, something inside of me clicked. I would sometimes go through two or three books a week. And once I got into that reading groove, my mind was set on fire!

First, I started with the autobiography of Malcolm X, then Ralph Ellison's *The Invisible Man*. I would later be inspired by more diverse books such as *Four Agreements, Wisdom of The Ages*, and *The Art of War*. I also dove into books about business and entrepreneurship like *Think and Grow Rich* and *Rich Dad Poor Dad* and other books on self-help.

But the books I give the most credit for setting my mind free were books about Black history and awareness, such as *The Destruction of Black Civilization, Isis Papers*, and *Black Men Obsolete Single And Dangerous*. And there were two influential authors that really inspired me; Na'im Akbar, *Vision For Black Men*, and Dr. Jawanza Kunjufu, *Conspiracy to Destroy Black Boys*.

Man, when I tell you I was living in another dimension, believe me, it was real—in my mind. All that information transported me to a different reality and a new world of possibilities. The reason why I'm sharing this story with all of you is that I want to inspire more people to read books and free their minds from the social norms that turn us into nothing more than robotic consumers.

Since unplugging from the matrix, my taste in music, television programs, friends, and the type of partners I pursue for a relationship has completely changed. I trained my mind to wonder, imagine, and create. You can't free your mind if all you do is absorb nonsense, reflect on the good ole days, and deal with stagnant people. I don't know about you, but I have a hard time connecting with people from my past because many of them are in the same place with the same mindset they had ten, fifteen, or even twenty years ago. They listen to the same music, talk about the same topics, dine at the same restaurants, and travel to the same destinations. I mean, how many trips can you take to Las Vegas, Atlanta, and Jamaica? Personally, if I'm not getting a stamp on my passport, I don't feel like I'm really traveling.

Freeing your mind also means freedom from routine and stepping outside your comfort zone. You have to train yourself to turn off your television and read a book, get off social media and travel overseas, turn off the old-school music, and check out these talented young artists like Mesago, FKJ, H.E.R, Mahalia, and Tom Misch. And start asking questions about why you think the way you do and believe what you believe. Do you believe what you believe because you went on your own journey and discovered the truth for yourself? Or did you take the Blue Pill and accepted the reality you were sold? Have the courage to take the Red Pill—question everything!

BECOMING A FREE THINKER

Becoming a freethinker scares the hell out of most people! We've grown so accustomed to systems or programs of how to think and divine books that dictate how we're supposed to live our lives that we've forgotten how to think for ourselves. Most people seek permission from social groups, family members, institutions, or religious leaders to determine how they approach their relationships, even how they practice their sex life!

Being the consummate troublemaker as a child, I developed a habit of questioning everything that didn't make sense to me. Unlike most children who kept their mouths shut and just thought it, I had no impulse control! I would just blurt out whatever was on my mind. Don't laugh. I know some of you can relate!

And although this mentality caused me to get a lot of asswhippings as a child and to lose a great deal of money in my business dealing, I kept insisting on intelligent answers to my questions. Whether I was in front of teachers, superior officers in the Air Force, or CEOs of major television and radio networks, if I had a question about why something is being done a certain way, I would ask, "Why?" You would've thought my name was Michael "Why" Baisden!

So, when people tell me they live under certain rules or follow the direction of a religious leader, my impulse is to ask them, "Why?" Why are you allowing that person to decide how you live? More profoundly, what authority does anyone in the world bring to the table, and what credentials do they possess that give them the right to dictate to me how I move, love, and live the only life I will ever have? Excuse my French but "Fuck that!" And to be even franker, "Fuck them!"

While I think it can be beneficial to study theology, attend religious institutions, follow the teaching of gurus, and take lessons from religious texts, the objective should be to process all the information and then apply it to the vision that you create for your own life, not to take everything literally, and to adopt someone else's way of thinking! That's not a religious institution; that's a cult! True teachers and mentors should teach you how to think, not what to think.

And what's so slick about these "institutions" and their leaders is there's always a scheme that requires you to make a regular donation which benefits them financially. And to add insult to injury, nine times out of ten, the philosophy they're pushing isn't significantly improving the integrity of these so-called leaders or their congregations. I haven't seen any evidence that the level of uncollected child support, infidelity, or domestic violence is any lover for churchgoers and preachers. To use a religious expression, I judge the tree by the fruit. Or let me put it in street terminology being from the South Side of Chicago, "Game recognize game!"

FREEDOM FROM ORGANIZED RELIGION

Like most of you, I grew up believing in God, Jesus, the Holy Ghost, the Bible, and of course, the story of Moses. One of my favorite movies as a child was the *Ten Commandments*. Charlton Heston and Yul Brynner played those roles so magnificently that if I saw them walking down the street in plain clothes, I would've sworn they were the real Moses and

King Ramses. I loved those stories! They were inspirational and so believable!

But then something happened in my twenties! I began to challenge myself with the same blunt questions I used to challenge others with. In other words, I started to question why I believed what I believed. I asked myself, "Why did I believe literally in the Bible, and why did I believe in God?"

I didn't stop believing right away. In fact, it wasn't until many years later that I began identifying as agnostic. But there had always been some doubt in the back of my mind that I was subconsciously burying. It wasn't because of sexual abuse by a pastor, which happens far too often. My doubt was caused by a phase I went through during my freshman year of high school, where I became interested in understanding the Bible, which led me to join what I later discovered was a hypocritical church.

The memories of that church experience, coupled with my insatiable passion for reading and whatever else was happening in my life then, prompted me to ask profound questions that had been festering for years. Not profound in the sense that they required theological expertise but profound in their simplicity, I would begin to engage people I knew were churchgoers by asking questions like, "Why didn't God step in to stop millions of my ancestors from the cruelty of slavery? And why did he allow slavery to last for hundreds of years? Why didn't he stop the Holocaust? Why doesn't he create enough food and water to feed the millions of children that go to bed hungry every night? And why didn't he stop all the pandemics and World Wars?"

When I didn't get the answers that made sense or any

answers at all, I began to question the biblical stories and God's existence altogether. I felt my questions were easy for anyone with any church experience to answer and certainly those who had been attending for decades. I honestly expected to be put in check and to go back to being a believer. But when their responses to these basic questions seemed unrealistic, my questions became more intense and intentional.

I would ask them, "Do you literally believe the world was populated by two people, Adam and Eve? Do you literally believe the story of Noah's Ark? How did all the animals from other continents cross the oceans to get to the Ark? And where are the remains of this Ark?" I went on....

"Why did God need a New Testament? Doesn't he know the future well enough to get it right the first time? Why are there commandments threatening people not to worship other gods but none against slavery, fair treatment of women, or child abuse? And where are the stories about dinosaurs in the Bible? Do you actually believe our planet, which is 4.5 billion-years-old, is only six thousand years ago and was created in six days? And finally, please tell me why does a God that supposedly created the universe need a power nap after six days of working on one planet?

My frustration with God's inaction was embodied in a quote by a 3rd-century philosopher, Epicurus. The modern-day translation reads:

Is God willing and to prevent evil, but not able? Then he's not powerful.

Is he able, but unwilling? Then he is not good.

Is he both able and willing? Then how can there be evil?

Is he neither able or willing? Then why call him God?

As I sit here writing and reflecting on this, I can feel myself getting upset thinking about the avalanche of unanswered questions. Not because I don't believe in God but because, like billions of people on the planet, I want to believe! Who doesn't want to believe there's an all-powerful being watching our backs twenty-four-seven, protecting us from bad things happening to us, loving us unconditionally, and inspiring us to do great things?!

But being a freethinker who always needs to know the "whys," I insisted on answers that made sense. One that I'm still waiting for my Christian friends to answer is, why is this God thing so complicated? All the God has to do is make a cameo appearance during the halftime show of the Super Bowl and put an end to whether he exists—once and for all.

But since there is no evidence of the existence of God, then it should be expected that people like me will have serious doubts. Of course, I would never try to convince my Christian friends and family members that God doesn't exist since there's no way I can prove that either. Besides, I have no interest in taking away anyone's beliefs.

However, I'm on a mission to promote transparency and free-thinking, and you can't free your mind without being truthful. To me, wishful thinking, not truth, allows people to scapegoat God by attributing everything that happens to it being "God's will!" instead of taking the initiative to do better and be accountable for their bad behavior. And I hold others accountable, not letting them use what I call the "God excuse!"

There's another popular Christian saying that goes, "God is in control!" But to me, that's a cop-out, and it keeps us from thinking for ourselves and taking responsibility for our actions and inactions. I know many of you believe that God empowers you, guides you, and produces results, and I would never try to convince you otherwise. But I was empowered by believing in myself. And I was guided and driven by my vision to be a better man. The moment I confessed to myself, not God, that my lies were hurting people and arresting my development, my transformation began.

Freeing myself from that guilt and taking steps every day to become more transparent has allowed me to have financial success, support my family, lead national protests, be instrumental in electing the first Black president and recruit a record number of mentors across the country for Big Brothers and Big Sisters. I can truly say I've lived an extraordinary life! And this all happened because I set out to do the right thing and worked my ass off—and I was relentless! There's no power on Earth greater than a free mind and self-determination.

You often hear Christians quote James 2:14-26. It reads, "Faith without works is dead!" Well, I have my own quote; "If you don't put in consistent work, EVERYTHING is dead, whether you have faith or not! And without belief in yourself and creating healthy business relationships, nothing you do will be sustainable."

John Donne wrote a poem titled *No Man Is An Island*. You should read it! But just the title of the poem itself is simple, just as powerful and inspirational as any Bible verse!

I hope that my words at least challenge you to free yourselves from the idea that there is only one source of inspiration, one source of love, and one source of salvation.

Suppose a man won't discipline himself to become his own

rescuer without looking to the sky for strength and approval but rather look within himself. Why should his success or generosity be celebrated since he's only doing good deeds to gain favor with a supreme being? Or as a reward in the afterlife? To me, the better man does what's right because it makes him feel good—and because it's simply the right thing to do! Can I get an amen?

ACCOUNTABILITY WILL SET YOU FREE

Regardless of your religious belief or non-belief, I think we can all relate to the Bible verse, "The truth will set you free!" Telling the truth is foundational in every culture to measure morality and build healthy relationships. And it's our struggle, as human beings, with the truth that is the motivation for me to write this book.

But people wrongfully assumed that the title, *Don't Lie To Me*, only applies to lies that our partners tell us about who they're sleeping with or the lies about their intentions. The point of this book is to place a mirror in front of you, the reader, to force you to discover the person who's really causing the most damage in your life—and that person is you!

Throughout this book, I've intentionally used the word "Transparency" repeatedly. It was my "not so subtle" way of screaming at the top of my voice. The truth that will set you free is your self-truth! And the person who is lying the most to you—is you!

Accountability is hard to face! I know because it took me thirty years to finally get it through my hard head that I was destroying women's lives, my reputation, and ruining my chance for a better life all because I couldn't be honest with myself. I hated myself for not being strong enough to tell women the truth about something as basic as wanting to have relationships with other women.

I really need everyone reading this to stop and think about just how much damage is caused by a single lie. Lies open people up emotionally to loving you. Meanwhile, the liar is not giving any consideration for how much trauma that person has been through from being hurt in the past—that's heartless! Lies set things into motion, such as moving in together, building relationships with their partner's children, family members, and friends, and making plans for the future, all the while knowing they're not the person they're representing themselves to be—that's narcissism.

And lies humiliate people and destroy their self-esteem for no other reason except the cheater is too petty and immature to be honest about having sex with other people, which is weak! And that's why I hated myself most when I was a liar, for being weak!

I'm sharing this part of my life with all of you because I want you, especially the men, to hear what accountability sounds like coming from a grown man! Setting yourself free starts with looking at yourself in the mirror, owning your mess, and taking responsibility for the damage your lies to others and your self-lies are causing. We can start by doing away with these dumb-ass cultural excuses for cheating, such as, "It's in a man's nature to cheat" and "A man is going to be a man!" What kind of fragernackle bull is that?

The truth is, some human beings are naturally more monogamous than others, but that has nothing to do with giving your word that you're not fucking other people! If you're non-monogamous, be man enough, or woman enough, to let your partner know and let them decide if they want to go down that road! Stop using nature to justify taking away someone's choice—that's weak!

But accountability is a two-way street. The person being lied to and cheated on, as well as the partner not getting what they want, must be transparent too. Allowing bad treatment and inconsistency only encourages more bad treatment and more inconsistency. Stop lying to yourself that you believe your partner will change because you know they won't! And for goodness' sake, stop lying to yourself that you're okay not being treated or loved in the way you need to be loved.

Speaking on that subject, I've always taken issues with this concept of people having different love languages. The idea is to understand that your partner may show love in ways different from what you expect or what you're used to. And this theory teaches that you should learn to accept that just because their "love language" is different from yours or unfamiliar that you should adapt because they're giving you all the love they have to give! Okay, I get it, and that's all good!

But to me, if that love language is incompatible with mine, then I have no need to try to interpret it, adapt to it, or understand it. I simply need to accept it and move on!

How does this relate to setting yourself free through accountability, you ask? Well, freedom comes in many forms; freedom to come and go as your please, freedom to be alone, freedom to change, freedom to be yourself, and the freedom to ask for what you want and need!

You are accountable for ensuring your happiness is your

priority and your responsibility, not anyone else's! And when we don't feel free to do and be all the things, I just mentioned that we're living incomplete lives, which, as I stated earlier, is living a lie!

Allowing society, an author, or an institution to convince you that you need to tolerate neglect, abuse, or simply settling for someone's best, even when their best isn't enough, is nonsense. My love language is not negotiable; we speak the same language or don't. At some point, you have to stop lying to yourself and be honest about needing what you know YOU NEED!

At the end of the day, the love language that ultimately matters is the unspoken language of what someone is not sharing and not doing. Inaction is just as clear a form of communication as action. If a person lacks initiative in an area central to your happiness, stop trying to decipher it; be honest with yourself, and accept it. Again, self-honesty is everything!

As someone who doesn't believe in wasting my time, or the time of others, I make my status and intentions known from day one—and so should you! There's no point in wasting people's time when you love in ways incompatible with what the other person needs.

Now, I'm not suggesting that people shouldn't be open to compromise, but you better be certain that your definition of compromise is the same as your partner's, just as Eartha Kitt's comment challenged us in the previous chapter by asking, "Compromise for what?"

If the thing you're being asked to compromise is essential to you, and you give it up, it's no longer compromising; it's settling! You may need to hear the words, "I love you!" You may need a partner who takes you out on dates regularly. As a man, you may need oral sex to be happy and satisfied. As a woman, you may need to be penetrated and handled properly and consistently to feel connected to your partner. You may need to live a poly lifestyle to be fulfilled. Or you may need an exclusive, monogamous relationship to feel secure!

Whatever "it" is you need, be still in your truth and don't allow anyone to talk you out of what you want! Once you evolve into true transparency, you will not settle—because you cannot settle! Your self-awareness and self-esteem won't allow it! None of us should be in the business of changing people's minds, and we damn sure shouldn't allow them to change ours!

And here's the most important part: communicate this to your partner before any emotional or sexual bonds are created so that everyone involved is informed and can make rational decisions that are mutually beneficial. Remember, healthy and mature adults want the other party to be happy, too, even if it means they have to walk away.

So, from this day forward, move with intention and be transparent about who you're involved with, having sex with, and how much time you're willing or able to invest. And then put that truth on the table like a Thanksgiving Turkey—from day one! Then challenge those who want to be in your space to dive in or say, "No, thank you! I'm a vegetarian!"

It's all about giving people a choice based on the truth! That's what transparency is all about!

Every new book is a journey into the unknown. You begin with an idea of the lessons you want to teach others but wind up learning more about yourself.

Here's to remaining curious and having the courage to fail, learn and grow!

19

CONCLUSION

I'd rather not call my last chapter the conclusion. It sounds so final. I understand writing one is a standard in the literary business, but I think a more appropriate title for my last thoughts would be "Until next time" or "I'll be back when I have more to say!" As a writer, there is never an end to topics to talk about, especially when it comes to relationships. There's only what's next! As with each book, every relationship is a continuous journey to push forward to uncover knowledge of self, which should be used to avoid making the same mistakes and creating more setbacks.

I don't know about you, but I don't have any more time for setbacks, do-overs, and restarts. I'm at a point in my life where I need to chalk up wins—at least for a few decades! And the way to start winning is to be "straight up" from day one about who you are and your intentions. And here's the most crucial part: you must make it crystal clear that you don't have time for foolishness!

Time is everything! It's the constant in everyone's life that never changes. It moves forward even if you don't. And mismanaging time keeps you from getting to what's next! You become stagnant, repeating the same bad habits and revisiting the same dead-end relationships, often with the same people.

I posted a commentary titled *20 Summers* that speaks to the value of time. It was one of the most popular posts ever on my social media platforms. The more I read it, the more I understand why it connected with so many people.

20 SUMMERS

If you're over 40, and certainly over 50, you've only got 20 good summers left before your most energetic and youthful years are behind you.

No matter how well you eat, exercise, and meditate, you're old after 70. Yes, you can be sexy, vibrant, and active, but your best body, mental sharpness, and sexual energy are behind you.

I'm writing this because I need you to focus on the reality of time! Eventually, we all age and move into a new chapter. But before we do, make damn sure you live life to the fullest!

Breathe the air in deeper, enjoy more sunsets, take scenic walks, laugh with more passion, love with intensity, create a tribe of like-minded people who "get you," and most importantly, see as much of this world as you can!

20 Summers may seem like a lot, but it's not! Hell, it seems like I was 30 years old yesterday, and now I'm in my 50s. Life happens so fast, doesn't it? Those years are gone, and our tomorrows have become so precious. The question is, how will we execute making them our best years?

The most important statements you can make to yourself when your days are done are, "I did that!", "I went there!", I tried that!"

So, stop procrastinating! Stamp that passport and delete anyone who doesn't add to you. Remember, you've only got 20 summers left...19 after this one.

Now get out there and really start living! Have a sense of urgency about how you spend your time...and be mindful of whom you invest your time in!

■ ■ ■

Of course, there's no way of knowing how many years we have left, but being a man of a certain age, the idea of only having 20 summers to live gave me a sense of urgency about my own life. But regardless of whatever age you are, the countdown has begun. The truth is we may not have 20 days, let alone 20 summers. Once you embrace that reality of time, you begin to deal with people differently. You come at people "straight up" about what you want, you guard your peace, and you are quick to check someone if they are mistreating you.

The title of this book, *Don't Lie To Me!*, is not meant to be a whiny complaint after the fact of being lied to or cheated on but a serious warning not to disturb your groove or waste your valuable time in the first place!

And don't even think about second and third strikes. One strike, and you're out! Once you adopt the philosophy of only having 20 summers, you'll insist on a return on your investment of time, and that, for most people, is happiness, peace of mind, and harmony. Love isn't more important, and neither is friendship, not even family. Most of us have paid our dues by raising children, supporting partners, and taking care of our parents. It's our time now! And we have to cease it selfishly! We must create and stay in our happy place or, as I like to refer to it, stay in that positive vortex. And that requires constantly being true to yourself and transparent with everyone in your life!

Life teaches us that unbelievable joy and devastating pain often come in waves. We've all gone through phases in our lives where we experienced bad luck that seemed to go on forever! But when you "live right," you can create a vortex of good fortune where everything goes your way. Great opportunities constantly present themselves, you're in good health and feel optimistic about the future, and you start meeting new people that get you! It's a high you never want to come down from. And guess what, you don't have to! All that's required to stay in the vortex is to keep all the negative energy out!

And nothing creates more negative energy than lies. Lies create uncertainty, and uncertainty creates insecurity. Lies generate negative momentum toward drama that will destroy your groove and pull you away from your vortex of manifestation. So, instead of celebrating one of our last 20 summers, we're distracted by inconsistencies and humiliating games.

My very first words in this book were, "Lying is a form of abuse," and I meant it! But not only emotional and mental abuse but an abuse of our time. Until the liars, and those who tolerate lies, accept that truth and correct their behavior, this vicious cycle of games, distractions, and time-wasting will continue.

If you're serious about continuing your journey to "What's Next," you must take accountability for the energy you put into the universe and what you accept. You must overcome your fear of losing people who don't care about losing you. You have to stop procrastination and do the self-work that needs to be done to get into, and stay in, your vortex! And above all else, you have to accept that some people are simply incapable of giving you the love you need and deserve.

There's a popular song by Lauren Hill titled Doo Wop (That Thing). The lyrics go, *"How you gonna win when you aint' right within?"* To me, these words are a challenge to do the work to be a better person but also to recognize that maybe you're not getting what you want or winning because your spirit and intentions aren't "right!" So, don't lie to people about who you truly are or what you really want—if you want to win!

Now that this book is finished, I can get to work making sure I'm "right within" and practicing what I preach. Every day I work on producing a life that I can be proud of and honestly share with others. Being conscious of the truthful stories others share about their encounters with you is a great exercise. It raises your awareness of your behavior in relationships and makes you more considerate of how you treat people in general.

When I travel to South Africa and Ghana in a few weeks, I'll consider adding to my own story. It's where I like to go to reflect and channel positive energy into my vortex. Ghana and its people connect me to my ancestors, Johannesburg inspires the revolutionary in me with the story of Mandela and the South African people's struggle against Apartheid. And Cape Town serves as a constant reminder of the beauty and magnificence of the African continent with its towering cliffs overlooking the vast breathtaking blue water where the Atlantic and Indian Oceans intersection.

Just thinking about it gave me an idea, I'm going to take a photo while standing at the summit of Tabletop Mountain and post it on social media as an inspiration to those of you on your own journeys toward transparency.

Maybe I'll even use a photo from my trip to South African on the back of this book as a reminder to others, as well as myself, to treat life as an adventure and to passionately look forward to what's next!

COMMENTARIES

DICKED DOWN

Now that I've got your attention, I think it's fair to say most people prefer great sex to bad sex! But what happens when great sex is all you've got?

Yes, some relationships can survive with sex as the driving force; we've all been there! But is it really great sex if it's just about penetration?

People claim they're not emotionally involved when having casual sex, but sex by nature is pure emotions! Maybe not always possessive, but it's damn sure emotional if that shit is good!

Good Dick, just like good pussy, isn't just about length, girth, tightness, and wetness. It's about the depth of passion and, yes, emotions!

The real challenge for women today is to locate a Good Dick that's safe, drama free, and mentally stable! I mean, what's the point of getting Dicked Down if, after you Get Up, you're worrying about your sexual health, peace of mind, and safety?

So, tell these men to keep that "Good Dick" if it's not a transparent and healthy Dick!

Ain't nobody got time to exchange headaches for orgasms! GTFOH!

STOP SAYING "OPPOSITES ATTRACT."
THEY DON'T!

The idea that opposites attract is bull crap! It sounds clever, but in reality, it makes no sense. Try dating someone with opposite values or attitudes about sex, marriage, parenting, healthy lifestyle, religion, and cleanliness. The word we should be looking for is "compliment" or "compatible," not "opposite."

This brings me to my point: when things don't work out between couples, it's usually because they have opposite views on something of importance. The question is, why then do we torture ourselves over it ending?

Disappointed? Yes. Sad? Maybe. But devastated? Hell no! The only reason anyone should be crushed by losing a partner is when they have wasted valuable time and money, and their health has been impacted. Other than that, your attitude should be, "Thanks for the lesson. NEXT!"

I CHOOSE PEACE OVER LOVE

Love is often conditional and filled with expectations. Besides, I can genuinely like someone and cultivate love. But peace is peace! And without it, you don't sleep well and can't stay focused.

And for those who need our peace to be creative, being with a "peace thief" is not an option.

No matter how attracted someone is or how great the sex is, once you realize your peace will be disturbed, none of that matters!

And by the way, you always hear people preaching, "Women need to be their man's peace!" Well, men need to be their woman's peace too. #PeaceIsEverything

YOU BETTER LEARN TO FLIP THAT SWITCH!

People with bad intentions count on you to put up with their foolishness! And the only way to protect yourself from these narcissists is to dump their asses when they become inconsistent, disrespectful, or abusive!

Of course, I don't expect you to become emotionally detached robots, but you better be smart enough not to allow someone to damage you—especially after they continuously mishandle you!

It's not about being cold; it's about protecting yourself and not allowing some ass clown to waste your valuable time!

#FoolISeeYou 👀

LOSING YOURSELF!

We've all felt lost at some point in our lives! Sometimes, it's feeling lost in our relationships or our careers. Nothing causes more anxiety than the uncertainty of not knowing what's next!

Every day, we're bombarded with images of celebrity's extravagant lifestyles, sex, the perfect bodies, and the perfect couples—no wonder many people feel lost and "less than!" But the answer to finding yourself isn't having more; it's actually having less—less drama, fewer responsibilities, fewer expectations, less comparing ourselves to others, and less stuff!

I think you can only find yourself when you get rid of things and focus on yourself! Yes, people will call you selfish, but so what! Sometimes, you have to be selfish to find your SELF and love yourself!

WHAT KIND OF WOMAN DO YOU PRODUCE?

I think the measure of a man is what kind of woman he produces in his relationships. By that, I mean, how does he enhance her by bringing out the best of her character, sensuality, and talents?!

I think SOME men fail at producing good partners because they don't have the proper resources. I'm not just talking monetarily but in terms of possessing a vision, self-confidence, and a genuine desire to see her be better, regardless of whether they stay together or not!

And just like any great music producer, he knows that by bringing out the best in his artist, he elevates himself by demonstrating his skills as a creator to the world. And that, in turn, elevates his woman to a place where no other man can reach her!

If men want to experience women on another level, they must abandon this childish mindset of being players and aspire to become producers! Only then will relationships evolve, and we can start making beautiful music TOGETHER!

NOT BETTER, JUST DIFFERENT!

Too often, we are guilty of ruining good marriages and relationships over an affair with the hot new chic or strapping stud. It's typical to be excited over the "New Thing!" But is the new thing the best thing?

When you're immature, you allow your hormones to control you or, worse, destroy you. People have lost their jobs, businesses, and families chasing after sex or getting their egos stroked.

So, the next time you're tempted to sacrifice your peace of mind and livelihood over a piece of ass, remember that new will always be exciting but doesn't make it better.

WHY I NEVER FEEL LONELY

Being single, for me, doesn't mean I'm alone or lonely, and that's because I have good people in my life with whom I can talk, catch a movie, or discuss business.

Intimacy to me is about connections, not just penetration, so I'm stimulated on multiple levels just knowing people love me and learn from me as I learn from them! This group is the perfect example! People who rely on romantic relationships as the source of their happiness set themselves up for a life of disappointment. My joy comes from learning, new experiences, and helping others, not falling in love or acquiring stuff!

To me, being in love is a state of being, not something someone provides you with. Therefore, I'm always in love with myself, people like you who I touch, and the life I have cultivated. And anyone who flows into my life experiences that love. So there's no room for loneliness because love always exists in my space.

The time I am alone is not spent feeling lonely but used as an opportunity to relax, recharge, think creatively, and strategize! Who has time to feel lonely with so much to look forward to?

If you feel lonely because you are "by yourself," you'll certainly experience it in your relationships. It's not your partner's job to get rid of your loneliness or to make you happy, but to enhance the happiness you've already created!

WET YOUR MIND!

What do you want out of life? I want to be a resource to help you get it. What are your sexual fantasies? I'm open to trying almost anything to turn you on and keep our relationship hot!

What are your insecurities? Whatever it is, I accept you as you are, your past...your mistakes...your missteps.

I love how you look naked, even if you're uncomfortable with your imperfections. Let's work together to improve our reflection in the mirror, and we can both gain more confidence and stamina in the bedroom.

Allow me to lead you, not to have control over you but to make your life easier, as long as you promise to use that ease to support me and create more peace in our lives.

If you cook, I'll fix what's broken. If you clean daily, I'll ensure you have a maid twice a month to do the floors, windows, and oven. And if you rub my back, I'll rub yours. We both need pampering!

I'll make you feel special, elevate you, and make it obvious to the world you're happy and untouchable. Just make sure you have my back and keep my secrets.

And I'll go as long as you need me to until you explode in ecstasy, until you tremble, making it hard for you to think straight and knock you out!

And the foreplay will begin early that morning when I tell you on the way out the door, "I love and appreciate you," and rub you firmly on the ass.

So, is your mind wet yet?!

IS SEARCHING FOR "THE ONE" RUINING OUR CHANCE AT HAPPINESS?

We are programmed almost from birth to pursue that one person in the universe who is our perfect match, who was made for us! Whether it's Prince Charming in Cinderella or Neo in The Matrix, the search for "The One" is programmed into our psyche.

But this kind of programming creates almost impossible expectations for any partner to reach. They must have a certain look, be the right height, have the perfect skin complexion, and have just the right hair length. And they must give us butterflies; otherwise, it's not real, and they're not "The One" (Dun dun dun).

Don't get me wrong, I'm not suggesting we go back to arranged marriages, but I do know the path we're on is leading us down a path of loneliness and disappointment! Maybe we would be more fulfilled if we weren't looking for someone to complete us. Maybe we would feel less pressure if we didn't expect one person to provide us with EVERYTHING! That's another self-lie!

And you all know how I feel about the "Monogamy For All Mentality." At some point, we've got to accept that for everyone, the concept of loving one person forever is a recipe for perpetual infidelity!

Maybe the answer is to change how we view relationships on multiple levels! And that begins with searching for and discovering "The One" in you!

Happiness is not finding a partner who completes you but connecting with many dynamic people who challenge you to think for yourself and who set you free to discover more about yourself!

POLY ISN'T FOR EVERYONE, AND IT DOESN'T HAVE TO BE FOREVER

People have no idea what they're getting into when they talk about being Poly. Unlike open relationships, polyamory to me is not just about having sex with multiple people but establishing relationships. And that means consistently talking to more than one person, caring about more than one person, having the sexual energy for more than one person, and most importantly, if you're the man, providing for more than one woman.

The idea of being in a poly relationship sounds like a lot of fun until you actually have to deal with the relationship part of it. Even if you're practicing being solo poly, you're still involved with multiple people with needs. Hell, even dating comes with certain expectations, and it hasn't even been established that they'll be a relationship; you still must talk, go out on dates, and get to know each other. That alone can be exhausting.

However, I haven't heard many people in the poly world say that being poly isn't necessarily a permanent condition. You're not trapped in polyamory because you choose it today or at a certain stage in your life.

I know that people say they are non-monogamous by nature, but I think if you're intelligent, you adapt to who is in your life and make the necessary compensations. It's possible you could be happy in a monogamous relationship long term.

The key, I believe, is not to promise to be monogamous but to promise to communicate when you decide not to be so that your partner has a choice to stay or leave.

LOOK AT YOUR WOMAN
THROUGH ANOTHER MAN'S EYES

I think it's important not to forget your woman's attract-
iveness to other men. Always keep in your mind just how
much they desire her and how they stare at her breast and
gawk at her ass when she walks by. Look at your woman
from their point of view and think about how much they
would love to fuck her!

I don't mean to be crass; I just want you to think of the
primal reaction men have to your woman when she walks
into a room. Feel that passion and desire for her the way
they do. It will take your relationships and sex life to another
level!

Too often, we take our partners for granted, not realizing
what's old to us is brand new and exciting to the next man,
which is why I think it's important for a woman to dress like
she's single when she's out with her husband or her man.
Don't you want other men checking your woman out? I do!
Hell, the way I see it, if no one else is looking, I'm with the
wrong woman!

So, back to sex, you should make love to your woman in the
way you know dudes at the bar or the club would if they
could get their hands on her. Yes, romantic love is all good,
but a woman still wants to get f***ed by her man. Imagine
what that dude who was checking your woman at work or
walking down the street was thinking. When she walks into

a room, men probably turn to their buddies and say, "Man, if that were my woman, I would tear her ass up!"

And that should be your mindset every time you have sex with her! Remember, what's old to one man is brand new to another. Never forget that when you're checking out your woman coming out of the shower or when she's all dolled up for date night. Look at her through the eyes of a savage, just like other men do! That's how I get down, and so should you!

LONG DISTANCE RELATIONSHIPS: DO THEY WORK?

Let's keep it real; a long-distance relationship can only work if one person moves to the city where the other lives. Otherwise, it's not a long-distance relationship but a long-distance screwing. And who has time for that?

Relationships are hard enough without having to deal with the pressure, time, and expense of traveling. Not to mention, one or both people will likely continue to have sex and date other people, especially if there are no concrete plans to move to the same city.

Trust me, I realize how hard it is to find quality people with whom you're compatible, but you must ask yourself, "Is a long-distance relationship the answer?" I've never dated anyone long distance for any significant amount of time without a firm plan of coming together, and if children are involved, you better have your s*** together!

So, if you just want to date and have sex, save yourself the time, money, and aggravation of trying to hold onto someone by Skyping, texting, and occasional visits. You're better off dating locally...or at least within a two to four-hour driving radius. Since I'm in Miami, that means anyone north of Orlando is out of the question.

But seriously, people who are serious about being in a committed relationship will have a time frame in mind the minute they determine you meet their standards. If they tell you otherwise, they're playing games or just not ready.

I LIKE MY WOMEN WILD, CRAZY, AND UNINHIBITED

There's a saying amongst men, "Crazy women have the best pussy!" I used to agree with that! But the truth is crazy women may not necessarily have the best VAGINAS, but they make the best lovers! Allow me to explain!

Good Pussy is physiological. Great sex is wholistic! Great sex involves the physical response to penetrating, but it also encompasses her passions, nastiness, and willingness to surrender herself emotionally!

That's what I refer to as Crazy! That woman who, once she trusts you, allows herself to be transported into a sexual dimension where anything goes! She's high on Us! No weed or alcohol is required! (But always a welcomed enhancer) So, yes, kindness and class are essential, but I don't want a sane proper woman in bed. I want us to vibe in a state of craziness the moment she walks through the door!

#CrazyAndUnihinited

STOP GIVING YOUR LOVE UNCONDITIONALLY!

Unless we're talking about love for our children and immediate family, love should have all kinds of conditions, such as respect, transparency, loyalty, consistency, honest communication, maturity, and emotional intelligence. (Look that one up because it's important)

And the people most likely to fall for this ridiculous notion of "Unconditional Love" are kind-hearted women!

They are natural nurturers and still believe in that fantasy Hollywood type of love, at least when they're young. And men with bad intentions prey on that sweet optimism!

If we all agree that true love is kind, considerate, consistent, and transparent, then those should be the conditions to give our love or to stay in love, right?

Otherwise, the only love you've got coming is from a distance. Better yet, go kick rocks!

#UnconditionalMyAss

WHY ARE WE TRYING TO "OUT ALPHA" EACH OTHER?

Most people confuse control with leadership and quiet confidence with weakness! People today are too damn loud and too defensive about being hurt that they must constantly assert Alpha-ism when the reality is most people aren't leading shit!

Just because you have a degree or earn six figures doesn't mean you deserve leadership or respect! Focus on creating a vision for what you want, value cooperation, and above all else, stop talking and start executing!

Stop defining being an "Alpha" based on who has the most domineering personality and start to demonstrate the strength of compassion, value empathy, and encourage transparency.

All these "Alpha" proclamations are nothing more than insecurity, sexual frustration, and ego trippin'! Action speaks louder than words, true confidence is silent, and bringing people together to serve a common goal is more evolved than worrying about who stands above everyone, proclaiming, "I'm the Alpha!"

Please take a seat in the VERY back of the room! You look and sound ridiculous!

#AlphaMyAss

THINK LIKE A WOMAN

This ridiculous notion that women would be better off if they learned to "Think Like A Man" is bad advice! Men, by nature, are more selfish, immature, and reckless with the care of themselves and the welfare of others! How is that something to aspire to?

If anything, men should learn to think more like women! Women are MORE likely to put family first, MORE likely to be willing to work through hard times, MORE likely to remember landmark events in the relationship, and MORE likely to be faithful if they're truly in love and fulfilled! And LESS likely to allow their thoughts and insecurities to drive them to violence!

But what is most distinctive in how men and women think is that a woman is more thoughtful about her sexual health and, therefore, less likely to spread infection to a loving partner!

I emphasized "Loving Partner" because either sex can be trifling in a casual sex situation. But a man is more likely to have unprotected sex with a side piece they care nothing about and then go home and penetrate the woman they claim to respect and love, the mother of their children and a woman who trusts him implicitly!

I said, "more likely," so don't say I gave no responsibility to trifling women! But ask yourself, as a man, and be honest, would you trust and value a woman who thinks like you? Or one who thinks like a woman, specifically a lady?

And finally, if a woman is involved with a grown-ass man, why should she have to think like one?

SOMETIMES YOU OUTGROW PEOPLE

Do you remember the moment you realized you outgrew a close friend, coworker, family member, or partner? I do! More than once, and the experience is always bittersweet! On the one hand, you're excited that your life is moving in a new direction, but there's also a part of you that's sad because you know your relationship will never be the same!

Sometimes it happens when you start a business, get a promotion, graduate from college, travel the world, or meet someone who completely changes your outlook on life!

The change in you is so dramatic that everyone notices! They can literally feel you drifting away. Sometimes they panic and try to transform to get in sync with your metamorphosis, but that only makes it more apparent that you're in a different place! Your mindset has completely changed!

I'm at that point again in my personal development. From leaving the Airforce to driving CTA trains, fatherhood, dropping out of college, becoming a writer, national radio, hosting two TV shows, producing two stage plays, social activism, and revealing my atheism and polyamory, my journey towards transparency continues.

Traveling the world, moving to South Africa, and starting on my 8th book are taking me to new places mentally, emotionally, and, I would admit, spiritually because the depth of my awareness of what I don't know is profound.

DON'T LIE TO ME

I know many of you are going through your own sort of metamorphosis, and I want to encourage you to embrace it! Hell, pursue it! The process of outgrowing people is not only healthy but necessary to reach your full potential. And there's no depth of friendship, romantic love or amount of money more important than that!

Now, get out there and find yourself. Life is short, and time is of the essence.

MEN WHO CAN'T GET IT UP!

Erectile Dysfunction is no laughing matter; just ask men who suffer from it or their female partners. The ability to perform sexually is the definition of manhood for most men. Therefore, the inability to maintain an erection diminishes their confidence and creates all kinds of insecurities.

What's worse is that men's sex drive starts to decline after 30. Meanwhile, women over 40 are just getting started! The freak hasn't even been released yet! And after 50, forget about it! These ladies will blow your back out!

And then you have the problem of men ignoring the problem, which aggravates the woman who's willing to work through it! But how can things improve if men are unwilling to address the problem?

As a man who has experienced sexual complications due to my diabetes, I know what it's like to be unable to perform optimally. It really f***ks with you! And my issue was temporary! And it was unrelated to maintaining an erection, but it still had me trippin'!

I can't imagine what men who live with this daily must be going through! It impacts your psych so profoundly it can't help but negatively impact every aspect of the relationship!

Look, fellas, you can't make up enough excuses, compensate with enough gifts, or eat enough pussy to fix this problem!

But what you can do is improve your diet, exercise regularly, and get your checkups!

Women shouldn't be made to feel guilty for leaving a man who won't take the lead in his sexual health, especially after patiently waiting months or years for things to improve!

LET YOUR PARTNER DO
WHATEVER THEY WANT TO DO

Yes, I mean that literally! If your partner wants to stay out all night, you should want them to! If they want to be on social media flirting with the opposite sex, don't get in the way. And if they want to have sex with other people, accept it!

How else will you know who your partner truly is if you don't allow them to do what they really want to do all the time!? Hell, you should encourage it!

Does that mean you stay once you observe their behavior? Of course not! That's where choice comes into play. That's why it's critical that you allow people to be their authentic selves to determine if you're compatible or not.

Both men and women are guilty of trying to transform into the expectations of their partners instead of being determined to cultivate the best version of the relationship, wherever it leads them!

Talk to me, and share your desires and fantasies. I might be okay with you flirting with other people, having a relationship outside of ours, or even having another sex partner! Hell, I don't know until I'm presented with it!

None of us should want to be in a relationship where our partner is suppressing who they are or what they REALLY want to do.

My attitude is, be your true self, let me see HER and then I'll measure what you're offering to determine if you're worth me considering another version of our relationship.

Instead of endlessly dismantling relationships because our partners want to do something with someone else, focus on creating a partnership so dope that they'll never make a decision that diminishes what you have!

And that should be the only measure of whether you're okay with someone's conduct. Does it take away from your connection with that person, or does it add something?! Not whether it makes you uncomfortable!

JOURNEY TOWARDS TRANSPARENCY

It's sad that people waste so much time lying to their partners and themselves about who they are and what they want. Many times, those lies start with ignoring the impact of our trauma!

Look, I've never been molested, but I've dated many women who have. I've never been deep into religion, but I've seen the impact of how it can really f**k some people up, filling them with shame and guilt!

And I've never been cheated on, knowingly, but I've damaged plenty of women and left them scarred, so I know how impactful being cheated on can be on a person's ability to open up trust again!

It has taken me over 55 years to reach this level of transparency, and that journey began when I was thirty after cheating on my then-wife!

That experience made me aware of the damage that lies can cause and how being deceitful can arrest your development as a man!

Transparency is not a destination...it's a lifelong journey! I plan to write a book to share my experiences and other transparent people's stories about the work that goes into reaching a high level of honesty and openness!

But you'll never be on a path to transparency if you don't admit that you're in a stagnant place! Just like Alcoholics Anonymous, the first step to recovery is admission!

DOES MONOGAMY
BENEFIT MEN MORE THAN WOMEN?

I think most women are suckers for falling for monogamy! Unless that man is bringing everything to the table that she desires, and she chooses monogamy, then she should remain free to be involved with as many men as she desires! The same as men do!

Men often use monogamy as leverage to lock down women they otherwise would not attract without the promise of monogamy.

When women agree to be exclusive, they cut off every other man who could date them, provide financial support, provide companionship, provide great sex, be travel companions, men who inspire them, male mentors, and a host of other men who could be assets to her.

I'm not saying that women lose ALL the men in their lives once they agree to monogamy...but most often, they do! Many men are insecure and will insist that she let go of every man she's involved with.

How is that to a woman's benefit, especially if she's financially stable, has a healthy sex drive, doesn't have children, or doesn't have young children, and who doesn't "need a man"?! Women are letting men off the hook by agreeing to be exclusive when they're not offering half of what most women say they need!

DON'T LIE TO ME

I'm going to say something I've never said before; polyamory benefits women more than men!

So, ladies, think twice before you commit yourself to one man. Make sure he's offering more than just monogamy!

WOMEN MUST CHALLENGE MEN
TO BE TRANSPARENT PART 1

So, how does teaching transparency fall on the woman, you ask? Well, it's obvious men aren't going to do it! Unfortunately, not enough of us understand it's in our best interest to be open and honest, not just the women's. So, if women want the damage to stop NOW...then to hell with who's responsible. Let's just fix it!

It was a woman who challenged me to be transparent when I was in my mid 30s. Sure, I was honest, but not transparent! The lesson began when my girlfriend in Houston called while I was entertaining my partner in Los Angeles. I saw her name on the caller ID and politely excused myself.

Mind you, I told my LA partner who it was. After a short talk, I returned to the living room and joined her on the sofa as she was watching TV. In a calm but direct tone, she said "Don't do that." THAT, she explained, was me taking my call in secret! "It's what I don't know that bothers me!" she said.

Initially, I thought she was crazy! But she was challenging me to acknowledge them in front of each other! Her point was if I was being transparent, what was there to hide? And she was right. Not taking my call in front of her was a form of omission!

Look, ladies, either a man will step up to the challenge when you present it to him, or he won't! So, why not test his capacity to be transparent...from day one!

But for a woman to challenge a man with transparency, she must first be transparent with herself! Women are caught in a vicious cycle of failed relationships largely due to being disingenuous about who they are, what they expect, and their "ignore-ance" about the man's condition and mentality!

WOMEN MUST CHALLENGE MEN TO BE TRANSPARENT PART 2

Too often, men learn cheating from bad examples set by men in the family or knuckleheads at the barbershop who dish out horrible relationship advice at every weekly haircut!

Yes, we need more responsible men to be good role models for our young men, but women can't wait on that, so they'll have to create transparent men or, at the very least, encourage them!

In my last commentary, I told the story about how a previous girlfriend encouraged me to be transparent, and if you ladies want to improve relationships, you'll have to do the same!

Believe it or not, most men have experienced being honest, usually with women they don't care about losing. Now, only if they could learn to apply that same boldness to the ones they want to keep!

Understanding which men are worth investing energy into comes down to what I said in the previous commentary; understanding his condition and knowing his mentality.

A man's condition is defined by what he's gone through in his life, whether it's abandonment or other trauma, such as being cheated on himself or sexual abuse. His mentality is defined by how he's managed his trauma, and has he set goals and then executed them? It makes no sense to invest in a man who hasn't been "Response-Able" or overcome his own demons and then try to challenge him with integrity. It's a foolish waste of time!

But assuming he's been able to tackle his shortcomings and if you're truly compatible, then why not challenge him with transparency to step up and be a better man?!

Again, I know this job should fall on fathers and mentors, but just as you took the lead in raising sons, you'll have to initiate the conversation about transparency. Not because you're desperate but because it's in your self-interest!

THE FEAR OF BEING ALONE

We're social creatures, so we are not designed to be alone. But when you allow fear to take over, poor choices usually follow.

A narcissist can sense desperation like a wolf smells blood. Some of you have lowered your standards, ruined your finances, and likely been abused by someone who took advantage of your loneliness!

Until you learn to embrace being alone, I mean, look forward to it, you'll always leave yourself open for manipulation.

Stop telling people everything you want in a partner! Narcissists will morph into everything you describe and love bomb you to death!

Learn to use alone time to do the work on yourself that boost self-esteem! But most importantly, learn to love being with YOU! Hell, I rush home when I'm out! I shut my front door and lock it like a fuckin' vault! Because I'm my best company, and I love chillin' with me!

Master that, and everyone who comes into your space will be forced to enhance it!

YOU'RE ENOUGH...FOR THE RIGHT PERSON!

It's sad how we waste so much time wondering if someone will like us, be attracted to us, or accept us.

All any of us can do is be ourselves, ideally our best selves, and then let the chips fall! But if all you have to offer is good looks, money, or some other tangible quality, then you're not offering much! We've all dated attractive people and accomplished people...and it wasn't enough!

People of depth seek other deep people. And those who are transparent crave the company of others without hidden agendas!

I think being at peace is enough, being authentic is enough, and being mentally healthy is enough! Once you decide what you offer is valuable, you'll attract those who appreciate it.

Stop wasting time and energy trying to be appealing. Instead, be more introspective and satisfied with who you are! That's enough...for those who are meant for you.

ARE MOST PEOPLE EVEN F**KWORTHY?

Just think about how much effort goes into having sex with a new partner. You must get acquainted, make travel plans to hook up (because the person you want to f**k is always out of town, right?), get tested for STDs, and then meet up for sex. And that's the short version.

The long version is a lot more involved if you want to improve your chances of having a fulfilling "Booty Call." There's the "Sex Talk" to determine if you're sexually compatible. Is anal sex a deal-breaker? Does she swallow? Does he know if she's a squirter? Does she love or hate being fingered? And is dirty talk on or off the table? Just to name a few!

And after all that vetting, you still must determine if this person is being transparent about not being a cheater. Whew! It's enough to make your penis shrivel up into your drawers or dry up your vagina!

Members often comment about how hard it is to find compatible partners, but it's damn near impossible simply to find someone worthy of you taking the time, energy, and risk to just f**k!

YOUR PARTNER SHOULDN'T HAVE TO BE YOUR EVERYTHING

Your partner shouldn't have to be your "everything!" You should continue to have your interest and maintain friendships with both men and women. If you had close friends before the relationship started, they should remain friends if they respect your relationship.

We expect people to come into our lives and sweep us off our feet instead of expecting them to enhance the life we already have. It's about "Sharing our lives,"...not "Dismantling our lives."

You must "have a life" to have a life to share.

ALONE TOGETHER

The thought of living with someone can be terrifying, especially if you've grown accustomed to being alone.

Some of us have barely gotten our children out of the house, and the last thing we need is someone bringing their physical and emotional baggage into our space.

But living alone forever doesn't have to be the only option. Why not find ways to be alone...but together? Living under the same roof doesn't have to mean changing your routine, changing your vibe, or changing the room temperature. Okay, maybe you'll have to compromise on room temperature every now and then. But that's doable.

The true test of compatibility has more to do with how you navigate your daily lives rather than how much you love each other. Let's be honest: you can love someone and not be able to live with them.

Love doesn't settle the issue of sleep patterns, noise levels, having company, sleeping with the TV or fan on, or diet and workout habits, which become more important as you age.

And love damn sure doesn't fix the issue of lack of sexual chemistry. Living together will be a nightmare if you can't f**k through boring times and arguments. Agreed? (wink)

But imagine that you're compatible in all those areas. You both love watching good movies, smoking weed, love peace and quiet, eating healthily and have the same music vibe and pace of living. Oh, and you're both clean and messy! Cause having different cleaning habits will break you up in a heartbeat!

If you're on the same page or, as I like to say, operating on the same frequency, having your partner under the same roof doesn't only make life easier, it makes it better! Your companion is right there! Your lover is right there! Your friend is right there! And if you're lucky, your business partner is right there too!

But here's the best part: because we've all grown used to being alone, we can either sit on the sofa watching TV together or retreat to our separate spaces without either person trippin'! That's the joy of being alone...while doing it together!

EVERYBODY IS POLY

In too many cases, we expect our partners to be our everything! Everything financially, sexually, intellectually, and personality-wise.

Just imagine how much less stressful it would be if you only needed two or three qualities from your partner and someone else provided the other things that enhanced your happiness!

If you really think about it, we're actually poly in many ways without even realizing it. For example, we're poly emotionally because we have different friends who provide different levels of emotional support.

We're poly mentally because we have friends or partners who provide conversation on different levels.

And yes, some people are poly sexually because certain partners provide a different sexual experience. Some people connect with us on a deeper emotional level, while another partner may blow your back! 🔥 #CrazyChemistry

Look, I've said many times before that polyamory isn't for everyone! But I think it's fair to say that monogamy isn't either!

SIX FIGURE WOMEN NEED LOVE TOO

Some of the most beautiful and single women in world are successful ones! Not only do they intimidate SOME men with their looks but also because of their success!

It's a very different experience visiting a woman at her apartment then to drive through the gate of her housing community.

That's not to say that men aren't proud of their partners for living comfortably but some of my brothers tend to feel a sense of worthlessness!

And to be fair, successful women have every right to have high standards for their partners, I mean, why work that hard only to share it with someone with zero accomplishments.

And that's the key word, accomplishments, not money! There are many six figure women dating men who don't earn what they do, but those men are go getters, passionate, creative, and they still manage to inspire their higher earning partners!

So, let's take the focus off bank account balances and focus on compatibility. A man who travels extensively, read's insatiably, is active in the community, and has a talent he's cultivated is just as attractive as a man with a matching financial portfolio.

The great thing about being a woman with money is that it doesn't have to be the #1 criteria for a partner! Now, she can focus on seeking a man who is transparent and makes her laugh!

ROLLIN SOLO!
DO MOST PEOPLE FEEL BETTER OFF ALONE?

Statistically, there are more single people in the U.S. than ever! It seems more men and women are deciding they're better off without the responsibility and drama of a committed relationship.

And who could blame them, especially those over 40 who either have been married once or twice or have watched their friends and family's disastrous relationships?

But sometimes, being alone boils down to not finding a compatible partner. Once you reach a certain stage in life, nothing is more valuable than peace and security. Sadly, most relationships diminish your peace and rob you of your security with all the lies and inconsistencies.

I used to be a fan of marriage and relationships, but I've discovered that titles and the objective of "settling down" are doing more harm than good.

My focus now is on encouraging others to pursue happiness and transparency. Once you achieve those for yourself, everyone who enters your life will be judged by how they enhance it, not just by being present and offering a title!

I CHOOSE YOU

There's something about that right person, that special some-one, that makes you smile just thinking about them. You look forward to the next time you see them, talk to them, or read something they wrote. They may not be extraordinarily attractive, rich, or perfect in any way, but they're perfect for you.

Choosing good people to be in your life means no one forced you to be together. You weren't matched up or hooked up.

Chances are you weren't even looking for each other; it just happened. I don't mean that in a coincidental or even spiritual way. I think we attract certain energies into our universe based on what kind of energy we put out.

So, even when we don't think we're choosing, we really are. It's just subconscious. When we want something or someone's attention, we know how to get it, whether it's how we walk, dress, speak, smile, or when we send a friend request to someone on social media. We all, in some way, want to be connected.

I know I talk a lot about the fear of being alone and people learning to create their happiness, but we are social creators. We need contact with other human beings to feel alive, to feel relevant, and to feel love.

Every day, all of us who come to this page choose to have contact with one another, sometimes to be entertained, other times to be informed or inspired. In either case, I'm glad you choose me because I post my thoughts every day because I choose all of you.

You get me; you can relate to how I think, and you love a good debate. But challenging each other is how we get to the next level. So, hell, yes, I choose you. What man in his right mind would allow so many beautiful, intelligent, and open-minded women to go another day without feeling wanted and appreciated?

Thanks for giving me something special to look forward to every day, but most of all, thanks for being perfect for me! We click, you understand me, and in the end, that's why we choose each other!

CAN I LOVE YOU MY WAY?

I'm comfortable saying, "I love you!" because I have matured
to the point of accepting the responsibility that comes with
uttering those words.

But I hope you won't create expectations just because I confess
to loving you. I need you to allow me to love you based on
what love means...TO ME!

As I said, I accept RESPONSE-ABILITY for loving you, and I
will consistently demonstrate my love in a way that is clear and
without question. I'm even okay with your reciprocation being
conditional on my consistency! I gladly accept that challenge.

But here's what I need you to understand: if you want to be
loved authentically, then you have to allow me to be genuine in
how I express my love without comparing it to other couples
or past disappointments, or Reality TV love!

Just let me show you, baby!—without all the preconceived
notions and Hollywood caricatures of what love is supposed to
be.

Let's create our definition of love. Let's create our protocols
and boundaries! And let's allow our love to flow organically
and transparently!

Can we do that, baby? Can you trust me to love you my way?

MEN CRY IN THE DARK

In 1997, I released my first novel, *Men Cry In The Dark*. the sales went through the roof! There was even a stage play adapted from the book starring Allen Payne as Derrick and Richard Roundtree as his father!

The women loved it, but the men thought the title was "soft"! I mean, what man wants to admit that he cries, whether over a woman or when he experiences success or pain?

I cried my heart out the day I decided to quit my job to pursue my dream of becoming a writer! Stepping out on faith with no safety net when you have bills to pay and a child to feed takes courage...but it's also emotional as fuck! Some of you have been there!

I also cried recently when I realized that I hurt my daughter, my princess, during an argument that went too far! And, of course, I've cried when I've lost loved ones.

You see, being a man isn't about not feeling pain or holding back tears but embracing having emotions, being caring enough, and being secure enough to express when you're hurting and when you've hurt others!

I've never shared this before, but one of my biggest disappointments is my failure to get more men to read my books and commentaries—because my love for my brothers inspired me to start writing in the first place!

I want them to know it's okay to fail, it's okay to feel, and it's okay to cry, as long as those tears promote more maturity and transparency!

I'm still rooting for you, my brothers, to evolve beyond playing games and inconsistencies, take your place as leaders, and provide a safe place for our women to flourish and love deeper!

I have faith that you won't let me and our sisters down! I don't give a damn what society or some misguided women think—we need you!

WHY WOMEN NEED TO FEEL SAFE

All the great sex, status, muscles, and money in the world don't mean a damn thing to a woman if she doesn't feel safe! This fact isn't debatable or up for any discussion. Security, on multiple levels, is essential to allowing a woman to settle into you, adapt, and, yes, submit.

But how the hell can she do any of those things if she's unstable, restless, worried, and even afraid that what you're doing, or might do, can be a threat to her world?

Being muscular doesn't provide security if the man is disrespectful and a bully. That fool will mess around and get you both shot! Money isn't security if a man doesn't know how to manage it. And great sex is only great if a woman doesn't have to be concerned about her sexual health.

Fuck infatuation and fuck falling in love! A mature woman is going to insist on security first, and then the love will come. And that security must be provided consistently; otherwise, how would she feel safe enough to allow real love to grow?

Lies, more than anything else, make women feel unsafe, distrustful, and humiliated! Can we, as men, at least tell the truth about who we are and what our intentions are so that women can confidently settle in or start planning their getaways? We owe them that much, don't we?

ABOUT MICHAEL BAISDEN

Michael Baisden is one of the most influential radio person-alities in history! At the peak of his career, he could be heard by over eight million people in nearly 100 cities.

In 2007, he spearheaded the historic Jena 6 March! During his career he went on a 72-city bus tour to promote mentoring with his One Million Mentors Campaign, he was credited by President Obama's Campaign for being instrumental in his election and re-election, and Michael was the first and loudest national voice to sound the alarm on the Trayvon Martin killing!

Michael is also a New York Times best-selling author of seven books, two of which were adapted to stage plays, *Men Cry In The Dark* and *The Maintenance Man*. He also hosted two national TV shows, *Talk Or Walk* and *Baisden After Dark!*

Michael is now one of the leading voices promoting Transparent Relationships.

As a college dropout, ex-Air force Airman, Single Parent, and transit worker from the south side of Chicago, he wanted his life to mean something. That opportunity came when he stepped out on faith to live his dream of becoming a writer. That courageous step resulted in seven best-selling books with nearly two million in print, two of his titles being adapted into stage

plays playing to sold-out crowds across the U.S., and two national television shows.

Baisden is a noted speaker, TV talk show host, film producer, social activist, and philanthropist, and has been presented with numerous awards. He was honored by Big Brothers Big Sisters of America with the Michael Baisden Inspiration Award. The award named in his honor will be given in future years to people who are dedicating themselves to actively recruiting mentors. Michael believes that "books change lives" and he is living proof! Stay tuned to his next chapter as his legacy continues...

Find Michael on Facebook & Instagram: @MichaelBaisdenLive
Follow Michael on Twitter: @BaisdenLive
Subscribe To Michael's YouTube Channel:
@MichaelBaisdenLive

www.MingleCity.com

MICHAEL BAISDEN:

As one of the most influential personalities in the country, Michael has hosted sold out relationship seminars for more than 25 years and broadcast to over eight million listeners in over 100 cities nationwide as host of The Michael Baisden Radio Show. Recently, Michael stepped down from his radio program after 10 years to focus his attention on producing for film and television, mentoring and public speaking. For booking and more information go to: **MingleCity.com**

MICHAEL BAISDEN LIVE - YouTube Channel
Informative, Engaging ... Funny!

Michael Baisden Live is dedicated to producing quality video content that inspires, engages, and promotes healthy dialogue between men and women about relationships, sex, marriage, and family. Our goal is to inspire people to live better lives and to live their dreams. You will see videos ranging from how to start your own business to improving your sex life. Our speakers include doctors, authors and everyday people who have a message and a lesson to share. So, tell all of your friends to join us on this journey to learn, grow, and explore new ideas and to bring people of every race and social economical background together. No matter where you are on this planet, we're all family.

FIND OR FOLLOW MICHAEL
ON SOCIAL MEDIA

Find Michael on Facebook & Instagram: @MichaelBaisdenLive
Follow Michael on Twitter: @BaisdenLive
Subscribe To Michael's YouTube Channel:
@MichaelBaisdenLive
www.MingleCity.com

NEVER SATISFIED II:
HOW AND WHY MEN CHEAT

What do men want?
Why do they cheat?
Are they afraid of commitment?
Can they be satisfied with just one woman?
Do women want to hear the truth?

I wrote this book because I was sick and tired of scientific theories about why men do what they do. *Never Satisfied* is a collection of interviews about how men feel about sex, relationships and monogamy. Do men know what they want, and more importantly, will women listen?

Men expect woman to have it all, nice figure, sense of humor, master chef, and sex guru. But she must be careful not to be too whorish otherwise he will suspect her of foul play. "Where did you learn that trick?"

Insecure men are intimidated by sexually confident women!
— Michael Baisden

MEN CRY IN THE DARK

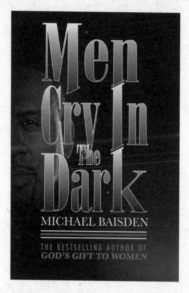

Men Cry In The Dark is an entertaining and realistic novel about fatherhood, interracial dating, and the fear of love and commitment from a man's perspective. Michael Baisden has courageously defied the stereotypes to prove once and for all that men love their children, cherish their women, and yes, even cry.

Michael Baisden is a Nationally Syndicated Radio Personality, TV Show Host, and Social Activist. He has dedicated his career to supporting mentoring programs and stirring up heated debate, both with equal passion.

"The truth will always be controversial; I just prefer not to hide from it!"

— Michael Baisden

THE MAINTENANCE MAN I
COLLECTOR'S EDITION

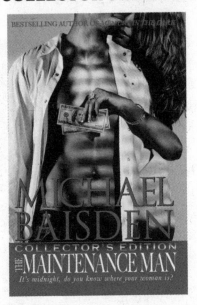

Every Woman's Dream: Malcolm Tremell is handsome, charismatic and a great lover; but in his world sex is not a game...it's serious business.

Every week his schedule is booked with secret rendezvous, extravagant dinners and sessions of passionate love making, all for the right price.

But Malcolm begins to reflect on his gigolo lifestyle when he meets Toni, a talented dancer and choreographer.

Would her love transform him into the man he wants to be and the man she needs to make both their lives complete?

MAINTENANCE MAN II
MONEY, POLITICS AND SEX ... EVERYONE HAS A PRICE

After years of being out of the gigolo lifestyle, Malcolm has to rebuild his list of contacts and high-end clientele. But he still has his good looks, his Rolodex, and his reputation. This time he vows that nothing will stand in his way of getting back on top and creating a franchise of escort services worldwide. He disguises his gigolo lifestyle as a nightclub owner in Miami — the perfect cover to mix business with pleasure.

BESTSELLING AUTHOR OF GOD'S GIFT TO WOMEN
MICHAEL BAISDEN

MAINTENANCE MAN II

MONEY, POLITICS, AND SEX: EVERYONE HAS A PRICE

But with high rewards come high risks. Malcolm's world is turned upside down when he begins a relationship with Alex Nelson, the wife of a powerful and corrupt U.S. Senator. When Alex and Malcolm are suspected of knowing too much about an unscrupulous billion-dollar deal they suddenly becomes targets. He will need all of his military training and street smarts to get his life back and to get revenge!

GOD'S GIFT TO WOMEN

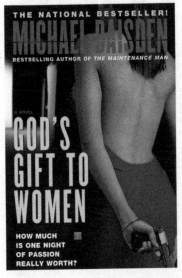

A smooth talker. An even better listener. And handsome as heaven on earth. He is *God's Gift to Women.*

Julian Payne gets into bed with millions of women every night. As an after-hours radio talk-show host, Julian captivates his female audience with his deep voice and sensitive spirit. Women can't get enough: They call in, begging for his advice about love, lust, commitment, and betrayal. Julian provides his listeners with the blunt male perspective, and he always has the right thing to say. But when it comes to his own romantic life, or lack thereof, he's at a loss for words.

A widower and father to ten-year-old Samantha, Julian wants nothing more than to settle down again with the right woman. Just when he thinks he's found her in Dr. Terri Ross — smart, stunning, and with her own counseling practice — Julian is confronted by a ghost from the past: Olivia Brown, a woman with whom he had a one-night stand. Suddenly Julian finds himself in a situation with a woman who's determined to win him over...or make his life a living hell.

Michael Baisden's hottest offering yet, *God's Gift to Women* is a compelling tale about the consequences of sex with a stranger.

RAISE YOUR
HAND IF YOU HAVE
ISSUES

IF YOU DIDN'T RAISE YOUR HAND YOU'RE **LYING** AND THAT'S AN **ISSUE**

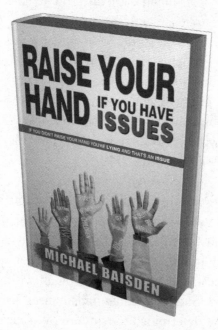

I'm Allergic to
Negative People

Dream Killers

Sleeping With The Enemy

There's Nothing Worse
Than A Liar

Affaiirs, Who's To Blame?

Being Single Is Not A
Disease

I'm Not The Same Person
You Married

Whatever Works

Fear Of Being Alone

Finding Your Purpose

"We all have issues, whether it's money, family, or relationships. But the biggest issue of all is not admitting you have issues!"

— *Michael Baisden*

WOMAN UP!

NEW YORK TIMES BEST SELLING AUTHOR
MICHAEL BAISDEN

LOVING YOURSELF ENOUGH TO BE ACCOUNTABLE AND ADMIT
THAT IT'S YOU THAT'S STANDING IN THE WAY OF YOUR HAPPINESS!

It's a woman's nature to nurture, but she must be wise enough to know the difference between supporting a man going through a tough spell and one broken beyond repair.

Yes, a man should leave if he cannot reciprocate his woman's love. But a woman has to love herself enough to know when she's being used and no longer valued!

Men invest in what they value and use what they only desire. Women must instinctively know the difference!

When you're happy in your relationship, you want to tell the world! But sometimes, keeping your mouth shut and staying in your bubble is better!

Finding a good man or woman isn't the hard part; it's finding a good man or woman . . . for you! Prepare, receive, and believe it can happen!

Congratulations
Michael Baisden
The *MOST* Influential Man In Radio